YOU KNOW YOU'RE A
MAXER WHEN...

YOU KNOW YOU'RE A MAXER WHEN...

Your stories in your words

As told by The MAX Members

ISBN: 1516875494
ISBN 13: 9781516875498

"This book is dedicated to the first thirty-two members who believed in me and enough to take a leap of faith to join me in this crazy adventure we call The MAX "

-Bryan Klein

Table of Contents

Introduction

Allow me to introduce myself, my name is JP Bartolomeo or just "JP". I am member 000000001. Before I get into this I would like to tell you a story about how a few cups of coffee and two guys transformed into a successful partnership.

In the summer of 2011 over four years ago, Bryan Klein and I met for coffee and chatted about nothing more than a vision. I'm proud and humbled to say this vision has spawned a way of life for tens of thousands of people around the country.

So the story goes like this –

My oldest son, Joseph, had been taking karate @ UTA since 2009. During this time our economy was struggling, however UTA was growing. On numerous occasions I watched Bryan engage his students in a fun manner while always encouraging them to raise their bar to the next level. One day I walked up to him and said "Hey I like how you run your business, would you mind if I bought you a coffee and pick your brain?" I know I took him off guard because of the way he tilted his head and cautiously said "sure". After we got strange looks from both of our wives respectively we met at Starbucks on Rt 9. We sat outside, drank some cold coffee and enjoyed sucking in the fumes from all the traffic going by at the speed of light. Little did we know this meeting would change our lives forever.

For those who know me know that I can talk, I mean really talk. I spoke first of course, and gave Bryan a background of my personal life, professional life, love life, shoe size, favorite movies, and love for working out and whatever else I could squeeze in before Bryan was able to get a word in. I explained that I had been working out most of my life and that I was a little apprehensive about a sprint triathlon that was next on my bucket list. Well, this was Bryan's chance; he said "sign up for it and do it". I am very happy with all the decisions I've made and consider myself to have a great life, I've always "Just done it". When Bryan said this it struck a chord with me; sometimes you just need to hear things a certain way. This moment of clarity and decisiveness gave me the encouragement to raise my bar and "just do it."

Now that I was completely out of breath, Bryan stepped in and said "I have an idea that I'd like to bounce off of you". He said "I want to start a fitness program; working out, nutrition & personal coaching." He had my attention, however I have heard these kind of pitches before, but I figured I at least owed him the opportunity to speak for a few minutes. After all, I spoke for almost an hour straight.

He started off with the workout plan as I was finally able to drink my coffee. He then said, "The plan is to workout 5 days a week for 10 weeks". I coughed loudly a few times after burning my mouth and then said "Whoa whoa whoa, nobody works out 5 days a week, it's not even healthy". I have been working out since I was 13 years old and was always told to give your body a rest. He asked if he could finish and at least humor him and his idea. So I rolled my eyes and shut my mouth. He then explained a quick overview of the nutrition program, food types, portion size, and portion times. The nutrition aspect was doable; however, I was still caught up on this 5 days for

10 weeks straight. Finally, there was the idea of coaching in an environment where accountability is not only the typical instructor-student perspective, but all the way down to classmates encouraging themselves.

I glanced across the table and said to myself "this guy is nuts," but he seems like a nice guy and I would hate to have his dreams shattered if no one shows up so I said something that has gone down in MAX History, "Has anyone joined yet?" He said "no". I said alright sign me up as long as I'm member 000000001. You see I wanted to hedge my bet that if no one else was crazy enough to show up and workout 50 times, I would be by default member #1. If somehow this hair brain scheme actually took off I wanted to give myself enough zeros to be able to tell this story. As of today we are in the 5 digit category. I guess my hedge worked out.

I am proud to say that since that meeting I have transformed my life on multiple levels. First I am 6' 3" tall and at the time of our meeting I was 243 lbs. I knew that I could stand to lose 10 lbs. but who had time to actually put the work in and get it done? Well we all have time for everyone else but seldom carve out time for ourselves. I needed to make it happen. I took the 6:00am class every day for 6 months straight. Right around 4 months my friend Bryan asked if I would be willing to take the reins and teach that 6:00am class. After very little hesitation and some great coaching from Bryan I became the 6:00am instructor for the next 2 years.

At about The MAX 1 year Anniversary Bryan approached me again and proposed he and I open a location in the next town over (Marlboro NJ). Again without much hesitation and great guidance we enlisted another MAX er (Randi Leib) to be our manager. We have just passed that 2 year anniversary and proud to say that we have one of our most successful franchisees.

So let's review, since I met with a bald guy named Bryan Klein I've worked out 5 days a week for the last 4 years (I do take some days off). I've taught a class almost every day for the last 3 ½ years (and personally changed the lives of hundreds of people). I own my own MAX location with my now partner Randi Leib. I've completed numerous triathlons including The New York Triathlon & Timberman ½ Ironman. I weigh 215 lbs. and couldn't be happier.

Amazing what a cup of coffee and taking advantage of the quote "Just do it!" did for me. Imagine the possibilities......

Take it to The MAX
JP

Member 0000000001

A little over a year ago, I felt like I was slowly falling apart. I was the heaviest I'd ever been, I was having issues with my back, eyes, skin, etc. and I had cholesterol issues. My cholesterol issues were different than most. My entire adult life I have had low HDL (good cholesterol), which also made my cholesterol ratio too high. While most people with cholesterol challenges have high LDL, there is no medicine for low HDL. I had been told the only things that can improve low HDL are diet and exercise. For years, I tried different things based on recommendations from doctors, and nothing moved the needle. Then we found out my wife was pregnant with our 3rd child and I realized that life was only going to get more hectic. I had a few months to make changes. It was now or never. I was exhausted all the time, so I didn't see how it would be possible to get up at 5:30am to exercise, but I decided to give it a shot. This was a 10-week program, so no matter how difficult it was, I could re-assess in 10 weeks. When I got the nutritional information, this program started to seem even more daunting. Food that I never touched in my life was required and 90% of what I ate was not compliant. Again, I told myself that I would go all-in for 10 weeks, and then reassess. Within 2 days of starting the program, I had eaten more broccoli than I had previously eaten cumulatively in my entire life. At the end of the first week, the scale said I was down 2 pounds, which was motivation to keep going. Each week that went by, I saw another 2 pounds and the motivation got stronger because the results were real. I lost 30 pounds in the first 15 weeks and have been able to maintain that weight through my first year. I am down 2+ pants sizes and am currently lighter, stronger and healthier than I've ever been. However, none of the changes in appearance or compliments from friends, family, and co-workers mean anything compared to the internal changes. After 6 months, I had some blood work and for the first time in my adult life, my HDL and cholesterol ratio was in the normal range! Additionally, I have more energy and the way I view food is completely different, as the MAX has given me the tools to make healthy eating my new norm. This is an unbelievable program with amazing instructors and even more amazing people that bring the energy and camaraderie every day. Take it to the MAX!

Neal Finkler

MAX Transformation Story #1

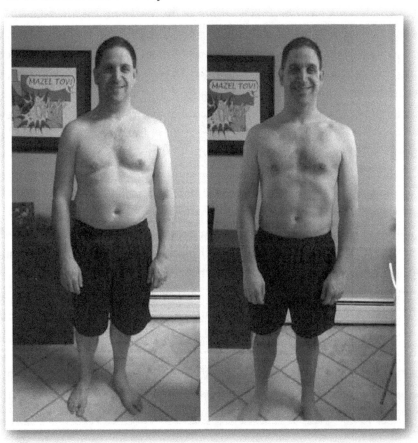

"The first positive change was after the first week!"
-Lisa M. Carolan, RN, MHA

I am currently almost done with Week 6 in my first challenge, and I feel amazing!! Had you told me two months ago that I would not be eating dairy, sugar and most flour products I would have told you that you were crazy. No way would I ever be able to stick to such a strict regime; and yet, here I am 6 weeks in and still being compliant to the MAX program.

The first positive change was after the first week. My husband told me that my snoring had decreased tremendously (and this was confirmed by my kids because apparently it carried throughout the entire 2nd floor of my house!) I truly believe this came from eliminating dairy from my diet. It had likely been causing me congestion and I wasn't even aware of it until I stopped consuming it.

I was hesitant to begin the program as I had knee surgery in December (the program started January 12). I had torn my menisci (both lateral and medial)-ironically, while doing squats! (I have since learned that I was doing them incorrectly. Kudos to the MAX instructors for showing me how to do this effective exercise safely!) I was attending physical therapy at the same time I started the MAX program. About three weeks in, the Physical Therapist said that I no longer had to continue my therapy as I was making such wonderful strides via my MAX classes! I have moderated the workout since day 1 as my surgeon told me to avoid high-impact exercise for now. Additionally, I can't do the exercises where we kneel down on our hands and knees. The instructors have been absolutely wonderful in showing me how to modify all of the exercises using chairs/wall as well as showing me how to make the cardio workout more low-impact. As such, my knee has improved so much! My range of motion has increased and I am able to do a more active cardio workout-not high-impact yet, but I am confident that will come in time.

I have a new found energy and my state of mind is clearer as well. I know this comes from nourishing my body properly in addition to committing to this regular exercise regime. We were measured by our instructor at the half-way point, and I am proud to say that I was down 7 inches. Also, I know that weigh-ins are discouraged, but it is something I do weekly out of habit. I am thrilled to say that I am down 17 lbs.! My overall goal is to lose 90 lbs. total, and I sincerely believe that I have finally found the program that will let me achieve this goal.

Lastly, I had my blood work done last week. I am proud to say that my A1C is now below the pre-diabetic range (in the past, I was pre-diabetic). Also, my cholesterol and triglycerides are in a safe, normal range. Again, this is definitely due to the MAX program.

Thank you for bringing this program to SIUH. Otherwise, I may not have ever tried it, and I am confident that this program that will enable me to reach my goal and more importantly, sustain a healthy lifestyle for the rest of my life.

Lisa M. Carolan, R.N.

MAX Transformation Story #2

> ## "I feel like I have my life back."
> ### -Victoria Mazza

My story is probably different than many of my fellow MAX ers. I am currently only five weeks into the ten week program, but I already consider myself to be one of the success stories.

I was never overweight. I was always fit and naturally muscular and lean. After 40, I realized I needed to put a little more effort into it though. I joined a gym, I worked out, not religiously, but enough to stay in shape, and I started to become more aware of what I ate.

When I was 54, having the time of my life, my husband was diagnosed with a terminal illness. My life stopped. I cared for him 24/7, and had the weight of the world on me. Everything from selling our house, moving, closing our business, and a thousand other life changes became my immediate responsibility along with taking care of a very sick and disabled man. For the next 21 months, until his death, my own health and well-being became the last thing I could think or care about. My husband passed away on December 3, 2013. I quickly descended into a deep, dark, depression.

There were days that I did not get out of bed. I couldn't sleep at night. I wasn't eating properly, and I was having a pity party for one every day of the week. I was drinking wine every night, by myself (that is soooo NOT me). I was eating ice cream out of the container nightly instead of cooking dinner for myself. I lost any muscle mass I had, and I looked like crap. Grief will do that to you. This whole ordeal aged me and I didn't like what I saw in the mirror. Then there were days that I would walk my dog around the neighborhood and come back winded. Sitting on the sofa for 18 months straight will do that to you. That's what really scared me.

My sister-in-law joined MAX of Hazlet in August 2014. She wanted to lose weight and get a better handle on her own health and well-being. MAX transformed her body, mind and spirit. Concerned about watching me vegetate since her brother passed away, she urged me to join MAX several times. I spoke to her one day in June 2015 about going on anti-depressants. I knew I needed to do something to start living again. Knowing how I had been a bit of a health nut for many years, she once again asked me to consider joining MAX. "Just give it a try....you will feel better, I promise you" she said. I started my first ten week challenge on June 29th, 2015.

Week one, day one. I thought I would have a heart attack. Honestly. It was the hardest thing I had done in a very long time. But I made a commitment, and kept telling myself I had to see it through. I didn't want to disappoint my sister-in-law, and I wanted to be happy again. I wanted to be healthy again. I wanted to get out of bed every morning and have somewhere to go. I wanted my kids to look at me and be proud of what I accomplished. I didn't want them worrying about me anymore. I realized it was time to start living my life again. At 57, I am not ready to stop living.

Today was week 5, day 2. I'm so proud of myself. I'm back on track with nutrition, I've eliminated sugar from my diet and I am starting to see the definition in my arms come back. My stomach is definitely flatter, and I wake up every morning without having to talk myself into going to class.

When I first joined, one of my sons said something to me that I think about every single day. It has become my mantra. "What is the most important day of the week to exercise? The answer is - the day that you are lying in bed, thinking 'I can't do this today'".

What I like about MAX is that there is a spirit in the room of unwavering support. The program works. I see what it did for my sister-in-law. It's gotten me out of bed, and has made me want to come back every day. I feel alive again, and want to look my best again. I am a work in progress, but I have made much progress already. For 18 months, there was very little that could get me out of bed in the morning. I am sleeping every night, through the night, and I am not winded anymore after a long walk or cleaning the house. I wake up refreshed and look forward to going to class. The sense of accomplishment is priceless, and I feel like I have my life back. It's truly amazing what just five weeks of dedicated exercise and proper nutrition can do to your mind, body, and spirit.

Victoria Mazza

MAX Transformation Story #3

"I didn't want to spend my 40th birthday feeling
ugly, old and miserable!"
-Priscilla Mcrae

I was holding off joining MAX for many months as I wasn't ready to give up eating the foods I loved and committing to the exercise regimen. But that all changed on my 39th birthday. I had one thought in mind - and that was I didn't want to spend my 40th birthday feeling ugly, old and miserable, which is what I was feeling that day. I had spent the last 6 years or so since having children - taking care of them and making sure their needs were met first. It was time I put myself first and commit to being a better version of me - the happy, confident me from my past. It felt selfish but I had to do it for me. I joined with hesitation but my weight had reached an all-time high, I was the heaviest I had ever been. And I was only getting heavier each passing year.

I had no expectations if it would work or it wouldn't, all I knew was I need to commit 100% to this if I'm spending this amount of money and I was determined to take this seriously. My first two weeks I remember feeling so sore I had to crawl to use the bathroom - I couldn't sit down, it seems funny now but it was that bad! I would put a small step stool in my shower so I could sit through the shower as I didn't have the energy left in me to stand after class. I would then crawl to my bed and lie down and I would literally set my alarm for when the kids got home from school, and I would pass out. It took every ounce of my energy to get up to get the kids off the bus after school. Oh boy was I exhausted, but it was the best feeling ever. I would step on the scales every morning, even though they told me not to. Every time I stepped on the scale, I had lost more weight. Some days it would be a few pounds, some days a half pound. The weight was literally falling off of me. I felt like I wasn't even on a diet, I was still eating, it was just regimented eating. I noticed by about the 4th week I wasn't modifying anymore and I could actually do mountain climbers and jumping jacks. The first time I ever did a burpee, a real burpee, I was so thrilled! What kept me going besides the incredible weight loss were the people. I loved the bond we had with my fellow classmates and I looked forward to seeing everyone each and every day. I started doubling class's every day after that point so I could befriend more people and I wanted to start working on my endurance to run a 5K. By the end of my first ten weeks, I was down 26lbs, and another 14lbs after that in my second challenge. I was voted as a finalist in that challenge and I remember how emotional I was getting that phone call when Maria called me to tell me I made it as a finalist. I was so proud of myself. I couldn't stop crying for the next few days. The day they announced the challenge winner, I remember thinking to myself to hold it all in, don't cry. Well, I won, and it was the best feeling ever. All the hard work had paid off. I can't believe the same old me that was a couch potato a few weeks ago was this MAX obsessed maniac who couldn't stay away from class each day. I lost a total of 67 lbs. in 3 challenges, that's just over 6 months!! From that point on, it was my mission to become an instructor and pay it forward. I want others to feel the same way I did. I fell in love with the people of MAX nation, with exercise and the feeling of accomplishment each time I ran a race, or overcame my obstacles. MAX taught me to always push my boundaries and keep striving to be better, to improve, and never give up. Since then I've run numerous 5Ks, 10Ks, mud runs, Tough Mudder and a triathlon. I'm a new, improved me and I couldn't be happier! Thank you MAX!

Priscilla Mcrae

MAX Transformation Story #4

Priscilla Mcrae, MAX Transformation Story #4– Before and After picture

After getting engaged in May of '14 my fiancée and I realized we didn't want to look back at our wedding pictures and be too wide to fit in them! I had heard about the MAX from friends on my Facebook page and thought they were nuts – working out 5 days a week? No cheese? No way. Then I saw how they were transforming. I called Roseann from the Staten Island Woodrow location that was in the middle of their first challenge on 4th of July weekend and she sat with this crazy person on the phone while on vacation telling me about the program and I said I would be in to sign both of us up (unbeknownst to my fiancée that is). We went in 2 weeks later to sign up for what I first was convinced I would never be able to do and now can't picture not doing.

I had gone for a physical 2 weeks before my September 8th start date and was well over 100 pounds overweight and had blood sugar of 5.8 and cholesterol levels of 190. I was told I was going to have to start medication and I told the doctor about the plan I was starting, we made an agreement that I would come in the day after Thanksgiving and redo the tests (what a motivator to stay compliant on National Eating Day!) I had lost 42 pounds at that point and my sugar level was 4.7 with a cholesterol level of 140 (still on high end but no need for medication).

Now I am in the middle of my second full challenge with sprint in between. I am down 54 pounds, and have lost a little over 20 inches. My wedding dress, which I was measured for in October then again in December was down 2 sizes at that point and will need to be brought

11

down another size before the wedding this May. My fiancée and I push each other to eat compliantly and go to class and even if we go soft on each other we don't expect our 8:45 PM family to let us off that easy! The reason the MAX works is the FAMILY aspect of it. I'll admit at first I was freaked thinking – are these people really that happy and clapping it up all the time? After the first week, once I could lift my arms again (J) I was right there clapping it up and cheering on my classmates as they were with me when I was finally able to do full sit-ups or hold my foot to my butt or even do more than 5 jumping jacks without moderating – which the first week I thought would never happen.

The lifestyle of MAX, once you get it down, realize you never want to go back to the person you were before. Roseann, Teressa and Michelle have helped us transform into version 2.0 of ourselves – smaller, faster and with less indigestion.

Christene Fossella

MAX Transformation story #5

"I have been inspired by so many people and I have been told many times that I have inspired others. "
-Donna Corris

I never really gave much thought about healthy eating or exercise. I was more concerned with my busy schedule of raising my family, work and on my medical condition of undifferentiated connective tissue disease. Most days I was in extreme pain and it consumed me. I was overweight and unmotivated. I eventually found a doctor in Philadelphia who helped me manage the disease.

My life was wonderful and filled with dreams of the future. Then "one day" (July 17, 2011) my world was turned upside down when my husband Tim suffered a massive stroke and died at the age of 54. He was the love of my life. We were supposed to grow old together. We had many plans and now they were all taken away in just "one day". My life would never be the same. Days were long and nights were even longer. I felt like a stone with no emotion and no future to look forward to.

"One day" in the spring of 2013 my friend Jessica Gondek introduced me to Amanda and Dinesh. They told me about the 10 Week MAX Challenge. They spoke with such enthusiasm that for just one minute I thought maybe this is what I needed to keep me busy and get my mind straight. I declined because I could not imagine working out, even though I knew deep down inside I really needed to get myself healthy in both mind and body.

Time went by and my life as a widow was the same. I was lonely and knew I needed to find a way to begin a new life. I remembered my conversation with Amanda and Dinesh and how enthused they were about MAX. I decided I wanted a new healthy/happy life and that was the day I joined MAX. Little did I know how easy it was going to be for me to make the 10 week commitment to MAX. I loved going each morning at 6:00 a.m. to workout with my new MAX friends who made me feel good. I followed the nutrition plan and gave it my all. I pushed myself physically to do things that I never thought I could. I even won the MAX Challenge. I can't fully explain the joy I felt when Amanda announced my name as the winner. My family and friends were all there to support me. They knew how much MAX meant to me and how it had become a big part of my new life.

There aren't enough words to express how grateful I am to my MAX family for all their love and support. I am honored to have such an amazing trainer, Beth Linder-Moss. She has showed me how to live a healthy/happy lifestyle. It amazes me that in just "one day" my life could be changed in so many ways as a result of MAX. I am very proud of myself and my accomplishments. In September 2014 I celebrated my 1 year MAX AVERSARY. My MAX journey has given me the strength that I needed to find my way in life. I have been inspired by so many people and I have been told many times that I have inspired others.

My life is now filled with happiness. I feel very blessed to have such a wonderful family that I love with all my heart. I also feel blessed to have so many friends that have supported me through these difficult years.

In just "one day" I learned how to love again and live!

Donna Corris, South Brunswick MAX Family

MAX Transformation story #6

"I wanted it and I went and got it!"
-Carl Nitti

My "success" with MAX is not necessarily measured with pounds and Inches but also with consistency, determination and the will to succeed in maintaining a long term healthy lifestyle. MAX has taught me so much in a short time in regards to Fitness and Healthy Eating but it has also taught me to trust in myself, that I can do anything and if I want it bad enough, it's up to me to make it happen. Well, I wanted it and I went and got it. After all, this is the longest I have ever consistently stuck with anything as I have in my 21 weeks with MAX other than work and my time with my future wife. I owe it all to MAX.

Before I started the MAX in September of 2014 I had let myself go too far in regards to Mind, Body and Health. Also, I had lost any self-confidence I had in my earlier years. Thanks to the MAX, 21 weeks later, I have finally regained confidence in myself as well as a new healthy lifestyle to go along with it. Not to mention also losing multiple Pounds and Inches in the process.

I owe a great deal of my "success" within MAX to my mates of the Staten Island /Woodrow 8:45 class for always looking out for me and each other and always being supportive of my plight since Day 1 of MAX. I also owe a great debt of gratitude to Roseanne Camarda and the Instructors for opening and running such an amazing program as they always go above and beyond to motivate you as well as teaching you the nutritional aspect of the program. As hard as it is to make this lifestyle change its a lot easier to do it when you are surrounded by an amazing cast of characters from the owner, instructors and fellow class mates on down.

Most of all, my success with MAX came down to one thing, the belief in myself that I can do it. Well, 21 weeks later I did it, and I will continue on this journey for as long as I am able to. Great people, Great Program, Great Results... Thank You MAX!

Carl Nitti

MAX Transformation story #7

> *"Not only do I look like a different person. I truly feel like a different person."*
> *-Stephanie Ware*

Looking at these two pictures. It's hard to believe that they were taken less than 21 weeks apart. The photo on the left was taken the week before I started my first challenge on June 16, 2014. I took the second picture on Nov 2, 2014.

Not only do I look like a different person. I truly feel like a different person. I am more confident. I walk with my head held high. I don't just admire the sleeveless dresses and blouses. I buy them. I'm not sure how many pairs of skinny jeans I currently own. But I'm wearing them out!! In June, the old me was buying MAX I dresses to cover up. I wouldn't even try on skinny jeans!!

I'm not done. I honestly don't even know how much weight I've lost on this challenge. I'll weigh myself on Sunday. Whatever the scale says. I'll be happy. Whether I reach my goal and maintain or continue this battle ... I know I have a lifelong ally in The MAX.

This much I know. The MAX works. IF you do your part. I've dieted before. I've lost weight. I've gained it back. I've gained back more than I had lost. I've exercised before. I've run a few 5Ks. But I've stopped. I made excuses.

I've never experienced a program like The MAX! I get up at 3:30am whether I'm going to work, going to a funeral, on vacation or even if I've called out sick. I'm committed to this program because this program is committed to me. The owners (Amy & Allison) are always there! In the gym, on the mat, and/or via text. I've never had to wait for a response from them. The trainers are inspirational!! Malcolm with his endless energy. Danielle with her endless motivation. And Melissa ... Mak is a spitfire that will inspire you to do things you never thought was possible. You can do ANYTHING for 15 seconds! Most importantly. The MAX Community is beyond inspirational! From the people in your class that you see every day. To those in your center that you see in passing. The Community at large on Facebook is refreshing. Whether it's recipes, success stories or setbacks. The MAX is like home.

Stephanie Ware

MAX Transformation story #8

Stephanie Ware, MAX Transformation story #8 – Before and After picture

"I'm making shopping lists, planning meals, thinking about new career goals."
- C.M.

Breathe. Breathe, breathe."...It's Hanna, my instructor's voice that I hear. My body is doing things I didn't think it could do but somehow it's doing it. I return to my trance like state. I know what a trance is because I am a Psychologist and I have had training in Hypnotherapy. Suddenly everyone is doing a different exercise, did I miss something. I say "Whatever, I'll just do what everyone else is doing and make believe I heard what she just said". "You got this", "give it your personal best". My trances keep interrupted by her constant encouragement. I try to stay focused on my instructor and the exercises but again my mind keeps drifting ....I'm making shopping lists, planning meals, thinking about new career goals. Before I know it, I'm thankful to be planking, I know this means the class is almost over and glad my body will be able to stop doing this crazy and foreign thing it's been doing the last 45 minutes.

Well almost 4 challenges later I can say signing up for MAX is one of the best choices I ever made for myself. It has improved my life emotionally and physically and I would even have to say financially. For starters following nutrition and attending classes has brought me two sizes and about 20 lbs. down.

In terms of benefiting me mentally, attending classes and have the support of instructors and classmates has boosted my confidence and has strengthened my belief in myself. One of my biggest accomplishments came during my second challenge. I decided to wean myself off a mild anti-anxiety/anti-depressive medication called Lexapro. I had been taking it over a decade. Knowing exercise was naturally increasing serotonin levels, I decided it was time to try and remove the medication which also produced serotonin. I am happy to say several challenges later, that this transition was successful. In fact, as I mentioned before, that trance-like state I go into has not only formulated the best shopping lists, it has helped me to consider broadening my career goals. During challenge 3, I decided to return to school and receive further certification as a Life Coach which I have already began to successfully utilize.

All I can say is that after countless plans to lose weight, this is the first one that has worked. But truly MAX is so much more that weight loss, along this journey I realize I got a handle on what is to be "physically and emotionally" healthy.

C.M.

MAX Transformation story #9

"Suddenly it was not about losing weight but about being a better me, healthy and full of life."
-Katie Belko

My MAX story begins long before I knew anything about MAX. In 2011, I was a nurse manager of an emergency department in a community hospital, with 24/7 responsibility for the clinical and business aspects of the department, also married with four young children a boy age 11, and three girls aged 8, and attending taking courses to finish up my Bachelors of Science in Nursing. Stressful busy life is probably an understatement. I was experiencing chest pains on and off for about six months when I finally went to a cardiologist to check them out. Long and short of that part of my story is I had a cardiac bypass procedure for a 99% blockage to a main artery in my heart. Commonly known as the "widow maker".

I spent all of 2012 reorganizing my life, changing positions in the hospital to have less stress, attempting to reduce stress at home, and I had made some exercise and dietary changes to my life. Those changes were made but they were not enough. An event like this in anyone's life can be life altering, and really shake you to the core. It makes you realize how precious and fragile life is. Even with all the realization it brings you to, it also brings another host of issues. Struggling with recovering from major surgery, and thankful to be alive to be with my children and husband, I was also suffering from depression, so much so that I was suicidal. I had been getting help and in therapy for a good year and besides my blood pressure, aspirin, and cholesterol medication, I was on antidepressants. I was at the bottom, even though I initially had lost 20 pounds I was not losing any more weight, and my exercise regimen was boring and not interesting me in the least. I was giving up.

In some of my therapy sessions my therapist shared with me this "new" program that he was doing, he told me about how he was getting up every day to work out at 6am and on this new nutrition program, he suggested I check it out. Initially I thought really just what I need a new "program", however each week I would show up at my session and notice a change in him, he looked healthy, was losing weight and generally feeling good. I continued to be frustrated that I could not get past my own self and be motivated to lose weight and get healthy in spite of the fact that I had cardiac bypass surgery and almost died!

So March 2013 I checked out The MAX website, and thought well this looks different, and the website didn't make any crazy promises, but said if want more information fill out this form. So I did, thinking "oh someone will get back to me in a week or so." Much to my surprise I received a call from Frank Baeli, owner of the Milltown/East Brunswick MAX in less than a day from my inquiry. Even more surprising to me was what I call the "non sell". Frank asked how he could help, so I asked him to tell me about MAX , he did just that, gave me the no frills, this is who we are; in 10 weeks we show you how to be healthy and help you do it your way and at your level. Of course not willing to commit right away I said I will think about it and call back. I can't really remember if I actually hung up and called back or if I just stayed on the phone, I just know that I made the decision of my life and signed up for my first 10 week challenge to start April 4th, 2013.

I was given information about attending the kickoff meeting, and I was not able to make the meeting at my center but was welcome to attend the one in Manalapan, I was skeptical, why did I need to attend a "kickoff", I would just follow the plan and I didn't need a group session, but little did I know that kickoff was probably one of the reasons for my success. I looked around at the people in that room and thought I'm not alone, so many others are here too. Then of course hearing Bryan Klein's story and the stories of other MAX ers success struck a chord in me. Then on my first day I walked in nervous and scared I was not really a group exercise person, and I wasn't sure I was going to be able to do this. Before the class started I was greeted by some of the nicest people I have ever met, they encouraged me to do only what I was comfortable doing and not to worry what others were doing. Well I survived and made each class that challenge. Exercise was embraced and I was showing up each day, and found that each day I was stronger, and doing more and more. For example I started my jumping jacks just by stepping out each side, by the end I was excited when I did 10 of them in a row, and really jumping up and down I was so excited.

Somewhere around week 6, I asked Frank, when you think I'll be able to do a real sit up. I was getting frustrated, and really feeling stronger and wanted to be better physically. Week 7 Friday, (I will never forget the day) I did it, a full sit up, I must have had some look on my face because Frank came over and asked, "What's wrong?" I said "I just did a sit up!" Frank without missing a beat says "do another" so I did, and then another, I think I did about 5 of them in a row that day. I felt so accomplished and so excited. Before the end of that challenge I went to Frank and shared with him some of my story, and through my tears, I told him about my depression and being suicidal and how in these few short weeks, my life had been changed, and I finally felt alive again, and I wanted to live. To many people I am not sure how significant the will to live is, but to someone who struggled to find a reason each day that was huge.

I had also embraced the nutrition, I was completely faithful to the plan, not straying except for a treat meal. My family couldn't understand it, but they were good as long as I didn't make them eat it too. I didn't I wasn't doing this for them, it was for me, and that was ok with them. I felt better every day physically and mentally. My clothes were loose and I was full of an energy I had never had before. Suddenly it was not about losing weight but about being a better me, healthy and full of life. Signing on as a legacy member was a no brainer. I did that without hesitation I knew I had found a program that helped me do what I needed to. To change my lifestyle, and embrace a new me.

Each new stage brought me to a new level of myself. What I had noticed as I moved through each stage was I was not only a better me with MAX. My professional life was better, my home life was better and my personal relationships were better. The support and encouragement I was getting at MAX was spilling over into other areas, I found myself seeing the positive in things, and encouraging others, giving high fives and congratulating them for all the small things. I have learned that it's the small things that add up to the big stuff. My physical accomplishments include losing about 50 pounds, countless inches, reducing my blood pressure and dose of medicine, reduced my cholesterol and medications and my antidepressants. I have also learned those numbers really are insignificant and the bigger picture is how I feel and what I can do.

My MAX life has had me run three 5K races, and I look forward to spring so I can run some more. I have signed up for a Mudderrella obstacle course run with fellow MAX ers, and another 5k or 2 during the year. I now have things on my bucket list like do a zip line, go cross country skiing, and other active things instead of a list of restaurants I want to visit. I have had my life refocused and I love to share what the MAX has done for me. My most favorite thing to do is share MAX with others, I have shared it at work and have several of my coworkers in MAX centers all over NJ and SI, I have also inspired family my brother and a niece are MAX ers too. Whenever a new challenge begins I get excited for the new transformations that are about to begin, and the endless possibilities that others will experience with the MAX. I enjoy sharing my story at kick off meetings, remembering each time that first kickoff where I was so inspired and attributed those stories to my success.

Katie Belko

MAX Transformation story #10

"The best place on earth is The MAX!"
-Pat Meli

You know when you hear people say the best place on earth is Disneyland? Well their wrong the best place on earth is The MAX of Woodrow!! I was looking for a program that was going to me help me when I looked in the mirror I didn't like what I saw. I hated how I looked. I hated the person looking back at me. After being a two time cancer survivor I wanted me back! If I could beat cancer losing weight should be a walk in the park. But for me it wasn't .then one day a friend I haven't seen in a while came by and she looked great! I asked her what she did and she told me all about the MAX of Woodrow.one sept morning I went with her met Roseann Camarda and she told me all about the program, answered all of my questions. I signed up right there on the spot and haven't missed a day since! After diets failing and the gym not working for me the MAX put a smile back on my face I started feeling like I had my life back .after four weeks of the program I was down 81/2 inches from a size 16 I drop to an 8. I feel great I look great! I'm always so happy. The instructors are the reason for all of this! Each and every one of them! They turn the word CAN'T into CAN. They really care about you. I have been there seven months I became a runner up for the first time. I truly believe in the MAX it really works! You have to work hard eat right and push yourself .the instructors help you through that. There more like a family somewhere you like waking up and going to. The MAX really is great it gave me my life back I can't say it enough times. The MAX we are all there for each other you don't find a place where both the owners' Roseann and Anthony Camarda are truly on board for you.so motivating always showing us that you can do it. I found my second home the MAX of Woodrow SI.

Pat Meli

MAX Transformation story #11

"I felt like a different person. I was 47 pounds lighter and my triglycerides dropped below 100!"
-Henry Velez

My name is Henry Velez and I'm a member of the East Windsor MAX.

I started MAX in September 2013. I was at a crossroad where my doctor had told me I needed to change my poor eating habits and lose weight, or I would have to go on medication to control my triglycerides that had reach over the 400 level. I chose to join MAX and to say no to the medication. By the end of the first week I didn't think I would make it through the end of the challenge. But every time that I thought of quitting, one of instructors or classmates would say just the right thing to keep me moving forward! By the sixth week I was doubling up on classes most of the days. The weight was coming off, energy level was improving, and I was feeling stronger with every class.

By the end of the 10th week, I FELT LIKE A DIFFERENT PERSON. I WAS 47lbs LIGHTER and MY TRIGLYCERIDES DROPPED BELOW 100. I could have never done it without the encouragement and support of the instructors and fellow MAX ers of East Windsor!

I'm now on my 70th week and people ask me "What keeps you going to the MAX ?" or "What's your end game?" I tell them there is no end game, it's a lifestyle change for me. This program and the people involved inspire me every day to stay disciplined and to keep striving to improve my nutritional and fitness!

Below are my before and after pictures. On the left is two weeks before starting MAX and on the right is one week after my first 10 week Challenge.

Henry Velez

MAX Transformation story #12

Henry Velez, MAX Transformation story #12 – Before and After picture

> **"I didn't know that I would be gaining a second family who inspires and pushes me every day."**
> *-Kristy Levine*

My name is Kristy. I'm a stay at home mom of three boys. Justin is 8, Jake is 6.5and Joseph is 2.5. As you can imagine, those 3 keep me busy. I've been an athlete my whole life, so I've always worked out. I've been to every gym and exercise program and I never got the results that I wanted. That was until I found the MAX. I took my 3 crazy boys to the Richmond County Fair over Labor Day weekend and I saw the MAX booth. I was so excited to enter the free challenge contest. Even though I never win anything I entered. I remember my boys saying, "Mommy why are you so excited you didn't win yet?" A week or so later I got the phone call saying that I won!!!!!! I couldn't believe it since I never win anything. I knew that this was going to be awesome!

I started my challenge in October and I have had AMAZING results! Halfway through I was like I can eat like this for 10 weeks. At that point I hadn't realize how this program has changed me. The workouts are so much fun and the members are like family. After the 1st challenge I couldn't imagine not continuing. It wasn't just a 10 week thing anymore - this was a lifestyle change and I was embracing it. I am more than halfway through my 2 challenge now and I am truly learning to like myself again. Being a mom of 3 took a toll on my body I gained 60 lbs. each with my first 2 and 70 with my last son. Today, I look and feel better than I did before my kids. I can't believe how this program has transformed my body and mind. So many people come up to me and say how good I look. I can honestly say that my arms have never looked so good. The combination of workouts and nutrition is like no other. I knew that good things were going to come out if winning that challenge but I didn't know that I would be gaining a second family who inspires and pushes me every day. I am so grateful that Roseann and Anthony Camarda brought the MAX to Staten Island. Everyday Roseann holds us accountable and reminds us that we can do anything we put our minds to and that there are NO excuses. She is ALWAYS there to help.

Clap it up for Staten Island Woodrow!!!!!

Kristy Levine

MAX Transformation story #13

"I have always battled my weight and tried everything available to shed pounds, but nothing ever really worked.
-Coleen

"Oh, wow," laughed the surprised middle school principal, "you look so young, I thought you were one of the students!"

"Oh no, you're the woman, who runs so fast!" grumbled one tennis player to another when meeting for a match, and "Your hard work and amazing results inspire me," said enough people to lose count.

To have those things spoken to me is an incredible feeling! At 5'4", 220 pounds, and 46 years old, the above quotes are not anything I ever dreamt I would hear said about me. I have always battled my weight and tried everything available to shed pounds, but nothing ever really worked. How many people have the same story? I decided that I would accept my fate and be fat and happy. Problem was I couldn't be happy... Not only did I hold back from doing many fun things, I became very much aware that I was compromising my health. I had no energy, but wasn't sleeping. Indigestion, reflux, migraines, and irritated skin, were some of the uncomfortable and worrisome issues I experienced. Very importantly, I was not being a good example to my children.

I am forever grateful to my friend, Maria Ragosa, for introducing me to the MAX Challenge. Maria had her own great success following the program and had recently become an instructor. She told me about the nutrition portion of the program and emphasized how it focuses on clean eating and eliminates processed foods. Maria invited me to try her class...

Shortly thereafter, I went. It was hard, but it was only 45 minutes, and I did it. "It's only ten weeks. I can commit to ten weeks," I thought and signed up right away.

I know it helped that I was mentally ready to commit to improving myself, but it was the MAX philosophy that was so influential to my success. Everything is broken down - it's only a 10-week program, it's only 45 minutes a day, it's only a 30 second exercise... Set a goal, and challenge yourself to take one step forward toward reaching that goal every day. I had a lot of work to do, but I set a goal that I thought was reasonably attainable – be 100% compliant in an effort to lose 10 pounds. At the beginning, I was so sore, but it was a good hurt. I was sleeping well, and had more energy. The nutrition plan was very satisfying. After two weeks passed, so did the indigestion, reflux, and migraines. My skin was no longer itchy. After over two years and many subsequent challenges, I am happy to say that those symptoms never came back, and I never want them to. My little successes led to larger successes. Within one year, I was able to shed 70 pounds and have been able to keep them off. I love my new lifestyle, and there is no turning back - I feel great and can enjoy an active life with my family! Thank you, MAX!

Coleen

MAX Transformation story #14

> "I will finally finish what I started so many years ago and not only will I benefit, but so will my family. "
> *-Stacey Alboum*

In 1988, I was 9 years old, a little chubby. At age 9, in the fourth grade, I went to Weight Watchers for the first time in my life. I sat among women of all ages and sizes and listened to them talk about their struggles and successes. At that young age, I had the courage to stand in front of the group and talk about how I had refused a cupcake at a classmate's party. This is one of my most vivid memories as a child. At 9, you shouldn't diet. At 9, you should play and learn. Although it was with good intentions, this experience set up a lifetime of horrible eating habits and an even worse relationship with food.

Through these bad habits, I continued to gain weight. I went back to Weight Watchers many times throughout my life. In high school and college, I was overweight. I never let my weight stop me from doing what I wanted to do, but it was something that I couldn't ignore. There were times I would try to diet, but by graduation, I was 250 pounds.

In my first year of teaching, I tried LA Weightless. I paid a lot of money, but it worked. I lost 91 pounds, I thought I had it. I stopped going and thought I would be fine on my own. Then I met my husband and after we were married, we were comfortable, we went out and had fun, and I stopped trying. Then I had my children, a daughter in July of 2010, and twins in June of 2013. In August 2013, I started seeing a nutritionist and started losing weight. I was 260 pounds.

Then on September 29, 2014, I walked into the MAX of Hamilton. I weighed 232 pounds. I was once very active but had not been in a long time,

I was nervous. I still harbored some old feelings towards food and saw it as a comfort. Then I started to change, yes I lost weight, but I was stronger, I was willing to try, I pushed myself. During my first challenge, I lost 24 pounds and felt amazing. I am currently in my second challenge, and have lost 41 pounds. I am healthier and happier with my appearance. I am still a work in progress and have a ways to go, but I know with the MAX, I will get there. I know this is different from any diet I have tried over the years. I have done two 5Ks, with plans to do more, and I am signed up for the Mudderella. The old me would never try these physical challenges, and now I approach them with confidence. The MAX is more than a workout and an eating plan, it's a life change and I'm so glad I made it. I will finally finish what I started so many years ago and not only will I benefit, but so will my family.

Stacey Alboum

MAX Transformation story #15

Stacey Alboum, MAX Transformation story #15 – Before and After picture

> ## "I need to be healthy to take care of my family."
> ### -Sindy Boldizar

I joined the MAX not because I needed to lose weight or because I didn't know how to eat. I joined because I was bored with my gym and wanted a change like I have every few months for years .I planned on staying for 10 weeks and then moving on. Well that was over 1 year ago! I am not going anywhere. I also love the nutrition and it's a bonus for my entire family. Although getting the veggies in my daughter is sometimes a work out alone .Every day I walk through the door learn something new it may be an exercise it may be a stretch or just how to work different body parts. I feel great, sleep awesome, gained muscle and lost inches.

I need to be healthy to take care of my family. If I don't take care of me I cannot take care of them. My son was diagnosed with Duchenne Muscular Dystrophy at the age of 2 1/2. A disease that effects 1 in 3,500 boys. It effects the muscles and the boys lose mobility by early teens and are in wheelchairs and they only live into their early 20's. My son is now 10 and needs help getting off the floor, getting into the car and in and out of the bathtub. He can walk no more than 1/2 a block. I have a wonderful supportive husband and a beautiful healthy 11 year old daughter who loves to cheer.

Because of the MAX I have another family. It brings tears to my eyes that these people I have known for a little of a year care so much about me and my family and push me every day to be my best. Such a bonus to staying fit and healthy! Especially my 9:30 Chicas and a special thanks to Dinesh & Esther

South Brunswick

Sindy Boldizar

MAX Transformation story #16

> *"I'm one of those people who has tried every diet and workout plan out there."*
> *-Ardena Dailey*

1 YEAR DIFFERENCE

I'm from the MAX of East Windsor and I wanted to share my story for your book. Here it goes:

I started my MAX journey because I'm one of those people who has tried every diet and workout plan out there. I was always looking for the quick fix. It took me a long time to realize I didn't gain weight overnight & I wasn't going to lose it overnight either. I joined a few gyms but always felt out of place. There's that horrible feeling working out beside someone who is fit and you are far from it. I have nothing against gyms but it wasn't the place for me. I saw an ad in the clipper magazine for The MAX Challenge & was okay maybe this is where I belong. I decided to join MAX because it seemed like they wanted to help you get healthy and feel better about yourself. I will be the first to say I didn't get serious with MAX until it was almost my 1 year anniversary being there and I wasn't getting the results I wanted. It has been almost 2 years since I started and I keep going because I love it. I love the trainers and all my workout buddies. We are all try to get healthy and feel better about ourselves. I can't say enough about the trainers they are all there to help ya in any way they can. I couldn't have done it without my hubby being on board. He has lost 60+ pounds just eating healthy. He doesn't have the time to work out. We started this new lifestyle March 30, 2014

Ardena Dailey

MAX Transformation story #17

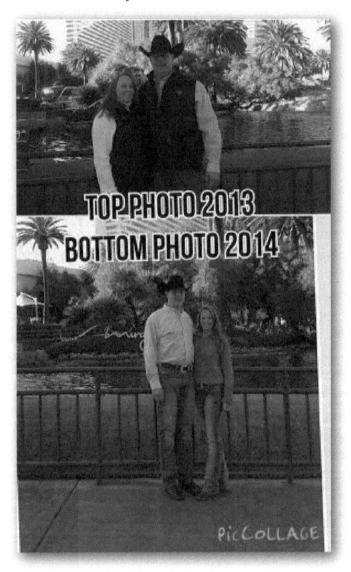

Ardena Dailey, MAX Transformation story #17 – Before and After

"I couldn't believe the transformation when I viewed my "after" photo."
-Regina Shannon

I love the MAX Program! For years, especially since I have had children I have struggled with my weight and eating habits. Through the years, I would lose and I would gain, I would exercise for a while and then I would stop. I was also a smoker. I was not inactive but I was not very active. For the last ten years, I just basically accepted my weight to be what it is. In November 2013 I decided it was time for me to get in shape, lose weight, and quit smoking become healthier all around. After all 50 is around the corner and I watched my mom struggle with diabetes in her later years of life and I didn't want to develop diabetes sooner than I needed to. I started going to a gym 3 sometimes 4 times a week. I ate good (well at the time I thought it was good still contained processed foods, dairy and sugar) and approximately 4 to 5 months later I was 25 pounds less and there I stayed. The scale never moved, my clothes size remained the same and I struggled blaming it on my age, menopause, etc.

Then, in the summer of 2014, my dearest and oldest friend Anne Marie passed along my phone number and the phone number of our mutual friend, Lisa, to Kate, the manager at the MAX of East Windsor. Anne Marie had joined the MAX of Old Bridge about a year earlier and she was enjoying a happier healthier lifestyle and looking great. I spoke with Kate and I thought "What do I have to lose?" I decided I would be more successful with the support of a group than I had been on my own. I froze my gym membership with plans to go back at the end of my ten week challenge. My friend Lisa and I were introduced to the program because of our mutual friend Anne Marie so we gave it a shot together. Based on our schedules, the 7:00 a.m. class worked the best. The class time was a challenge only because I am not a morning person. Lisa and I started to attend the 7:00 class regularly. I loved the exercise classes immediately, the motivation, encouragement and energy at these classes kept me going back every day. I couldn't believe I was getting out of bed that early in the morning with a smile on my face. The high fives and clapping it up was a little much in the beginning but soon I found myself doing that even outside of class and actually looked forward to high fiving and clapping it up during my morning class.

I was terrified of the nutrition but determined to understand the program. Like everyone else I have a very busy life, I work two jobs at least 3 days a work, and I do work 7 days a week. I have a husband and 2 kids and pets and a home to look after, how am I ever going to prepare, shop and cook my food. Not to mention, I don't cook. I have been married for 22 years and my husband is the cook of the family. He married the only Italian sister that didn't cook. I took a deep breath and I handled the nutrition one day at a time. The first 3 weeks, I thought I would never make it. I ate more food than I did on a normal basis. By week 5 I started to get the hang of it. I really enjoyed my treat meals in the beginning but after a while my treat meals became more of everything good instead of bad food. I pretty much began to eliminate dairy, sugar and processed foods even during my treat times. I didn't like the way I would feel the next day.

At the end of the first ten weeks I couldn't believe the transformation when I viewed my "after" photo, I actually cried. Do I really look like that? I felt young, energized and healthy. I never really looked in the mirror the entire time but I did feel my clothes become loser and not as tight. I didn't run home to get undressed at night, I enjoyed being dressed. I was a finalist in my first challenge and that was an awesome feeling. I had accomplished more than I had planned to do. I became an inspiration to others. We were all on this road together and I could help to lead the way.

I actually achieved what I set out to do for myself and I gained so much more than I anticipated. It was hard work but the reward was worth it.

The comments from family and friends were encouraging most of the time. At first, people were afraid to say anything to me I think they thought I was sick not that I looked sick but the weight loss was significant. In the 5 months it took me to lose the 25 pounds when I first began my journey it took 10 weeks at the MAX to lose 30 pounds and tone my body and increase my strength and energy. Oh yeah and my friend Anne Marie I told you about well she now owns a MAX in Woodbridge and asked me to be in an ad in the Woodbridge Smart Shopper for the Woodbridge location. She put me in 3 issues. I was glad I could repay her for introducing me to the MAX and encouraging me to join the program.

At the end of my first ten weeks and into the first part of the sprint, I knew it was time to quit smoking. I had reached a point during the exercise where I was not going to go further because I couldn't breathe not because I couldn't physically do it. So I quit smoking and took up running. I also hated to run, especially on a treadmill but I love running outside, I'm not the fastest runner and I am working my way up, I have done some little 3K, 5K runs and I am eventually hoping to run a half marathon by the end of 2015. I am smoke free almost three months now and I am so thankful I found the willpower to quit. I will be running my first 8K on April 12 and look forward to the finish line. I have set all kinds of fitness goals for myself for the year ahead which include a couple of mud races and runs.

I now enjoy cooking which I never did before. I am always at Shop Rite or a food store looking for healthy groceries. I love finding new recipes and learning how to cook good food. The MAX Facebook page is an excellent resource (before MAX I was not a face booker). I encouraged my husband to join and now he is a MAXer. Together we are learning to cook healthy and exercise daily.

This program works for so many reasons. Clean eating (which is so much better for your body) and the exercise program (which includes partner drills, cardio and strength training) are just some of the main reasons you see results. There is also the motivation and energy from the MAX instructors and fellow MAXers. Needless to say, I left my initial gym and have become a Legacy member of the MAX.

I just finished my second challenge and took my "after" photo today and I still see changes in my body. I'm down to a Size 6 from a Size 16, wearing Small tops not Extra Large to hide by tummy area and for the first time in a long time I can't wait to wear a bathing suit this summer. It's pretty amazing how this program just keeps working and working. I love the MAX and I encourage so many people to give it a try. People have told me because of my enthusiasm it has encouraged them to join. It makes me happy when they do. It's not for everyone but if you are willing to be open minded and change your lifestyle it works, I'm glad I found MAX.

Regina Shannon

MAX Transformation story #18

> ### "I was told: "you look thinner", "you look younger", and my favorite: "you look healthy!"
> ### -Paul Levine

I may not be your typical MAX success story because I was never the guy that people called overweight. For most of my life, I was the small framed skinny kid. I ran track and cross country in high school and back then I was in the best shape of my life. But that was over 20 years ago! The last few years as I approached "middle age" I started to see that typical male beer belly exponentially take on a life of its own. I also have family history of heart disease as my father passed away of a heart attack at only age 41 when I was only 13 years old. Now seemed like the best time to ensure that I'll be healthy for my 2 daughters Allysa and Lauren, and my wife Chris for years to come.

In November 2014, after seeing the bumper magnets all over town, I decided to take the FREE MAX sample class. If I liked it, I would sign up and start my new year's resolution in January. Well, I did the sample class and it was a blast so I signed up right on the spot for the special 4 week holiday "sprint challenge." In the first 2 weeks of following the MAX nutrition plan and coming to EVERY class, I lost 10 pounds! In the following 2 weeks, I lost 5 more for a total of 15 and counting!

Now, not only can I fit clothing that I had to put in the attic years ago, but I feel great! Everything is easier. Pushups, sit-ups, jumping jacks, and even running up and down the stairs in my house are all a lot simpler with that little bit of extra weight off my back. Now I look in the mirror and see a smaller face, smaller belly, and am starting to show some definition in my arms which is my ultimate goal.

At my company's annual sales conference in January, I saw co-workers that I hadn't seen since last year. On the first night at the reception dinner several people commented on how much better I looked! I was told: "you look thinner", "you look younger", and my favorite: "you look healthy!"

What they couldn't see were the changes on the inside. I just got blood work done and found out that since my last annual check-up my cholesterol is now down a whopping 95 points!

Looking forward to my next 10 week challenge with MAX, and fully expecting to look like that 17 year old cross country runner in the next 2-3 months!

Paul Levine

MAX Transformation story #19

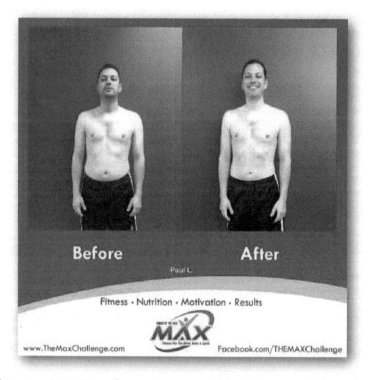

Paul Levine, MAX Transformation story #19 – Before and After picture

> "I warn you it becomes addictive where even that 5:10 AM alarm clock wake up does not sound that bad."
> *-Al LaGratta*

There are many reasons why I finally decided to join MAX. I have had many health issues in the past and currently such as: (my wife, Margie hates when I even tell it) Prostate Cancer, a left Mammary Artery Heart Robotic Bypass, A radical left Nephrectomy (removal of my left kidney) and currently there is a tumor on my right kidney. I have tried to remain positive throughout these issues and basically I have always been a positive person. Also I am a Type 2 Diabetic which does not help my cause since I am a Diabetes Marketing Specialist giving clinical results and talking about my products from AstraZeneca to many physicians in practices, hospitals and Speaker programs in my career.

The reason I mention all this is because of the results after 10 weeks with The MAX program. Overall lab results from blood work dramatically improved, Diabetic glucose and HAlc have improved, and I am sure the effect on Serotonin levels in the brain help to improve the overall good feeling and attitude.

Aside from the health reasons of why I joined I must give shout outs to MAX members Jessica Gondek and Donna Corris who urged me for almost a year to join, and seeing their amazing results and progress was another deciding factor. And last but not at all least my wife, Margie, said she would join for my support, and her fitness, and it has been a fun journey together.

Personally, I feel that many of us have tried diet programs with exercise in the past but none with these tremendous aspects and results. I have met a group in the South Brunswick 6AM class of very dedicated and supportive members and staff who are with you all the way with nutritional and fitness guidance. Our leader, trainer, and inspiration to myself and many others is Beth Linder Moss. Her style, approach, toughness, dedication, and her attitude every day is amazing and each class is different while she makes each session challenging and sometimes even "FUN?!!?" lol

Margie and I are looking forward to our next 10 week challenge and I would encourage anyone who would like to see a change in their overall health, attitude and looks to join. I warn you it becomes addictive where even that 5:10 AM alarm clock wake up does not sound that bad.

The MAX Challenge statements really say it all: FITNESS, NUTRITION, MOTIVATION, RESULTS for the MIND, BODY and SPIRIT!!!   Take it to the MAX!!!!

Al LaGratta

MAX Transformation story #20

> "I couldn't even bend down and tie my shoes so where was I going?"
> *-Faye*

FAYE'S LIFE CHANGING JOURNEY

The six years before I found The MAX had been the most difficult years of my life! I was facing one crisis after another. Most involved the people I loved the most, my husband, both my children and my parents. There were constant health issues and financial stresses and with each new challenge that arose, I needed to be strong and keep going. But each year, I gained at least 20 lbs. until finally I had reached a point where I would not be strong enough to take care of anyone. I refused to go to a doctor because I knew they would be weighing me and I just didn't need to hear it. But I could feel my body shutting down on me. Even the simplest everyday tasks had become almost impossible. I couldn't enjoy my family and I was so embarrassed by what I looked like that I avoided any social situations. I was becoming a bitter recluse. It wasn't until I saw my daughter starting to follow my lead that I knew something had to be done. But what? I couldn't afford a personal trainer. I already knew that the $19.99/month gym didn't work because no one cared, there was never any support there and I accomplished nothing in the past. I couldn't even bend down and tie my shoes so where was I going?

I decided that the only solution for me was bariatric surgery. I went as far as to schedule a date and began the process of getting cleared for surgery. During that process, I realized that this was not an easy way out and would require a huge amount of discipline and a drastic lifestyle change. I thought to myself, if I had this much discipline, I wouldn't need this surgery. I was even more uncertain about what I was planning. What if I got the surgery and then still couldn't control my eating and ended up with worse problems than before? I postponed the surgery because I was scared!!

Over the holiday season, as I usually did, I had gained even more weight. My friend told me about MAX and how she worked out every morning at 5am in Manalapan. I stopped her right there and gave her all my reasons for not going. It was too early, I was too out of shape and would drop dead if I tried to exercise and I would be too embarrassed to work out with people. I had all my excuses lined up, as I'm sure so many others have too.

I was stuck in a very bad place and just had no idea how I was going to get out. By now I was so depressed that I would get up, get the kids to school and go back to bed until noon. I did just enough to make it look acceptable but I knew that this was not going to end well without a huge change. So my friend tried again but this time she told me about Christine. She was instructing at 9am in Matawan and my friend convinced me to give it a try. After hearing Christine's story and seeing her transformation, I decided that it would be safe to go there. She would certainly understand if I could not do some of the exercises. I was still a nervous wreck and my friend came with me. Well Christine was not there and I met Evan.

Oh crap!! There was a class of 4 people, so there was nowhere to hide and now I have someone who people called Captain crazy pants teaching me!! What did I get myself into? We started with a little jogging in place. Ok I did it, not too bad. "In ten seconds, we are going into jumping jacks" said Evan. No problem, I thought. I used to do them all the time when I was younger. Well I could not do one. Not one jumping jack!!! My legs would not move! But this being MAX, that was not a problem. They showed me a modification and I was back in the game. I struggled with every other part of the warm up too but modified it all. I couldn't even grab my ankle for the stretching. It was bad!! But for some reason I wasn't embarrassed. I was determined to keep coming back until I could do it.

Since that date I have lost over 70 pounds. I am doing things I could never do before. I have even starting instructing classes now!! Talk about a complete transformation!!! People that meet me now would never believe where I started. I'm always so proud to show the people that knew me in the beginning what I can do now because honestly, it was their support and faith in me that gave me the motivation to do it!!

Just like Christine's story made me believe I could try this, I hope my story inspires someone else to take that first step. It's the hardest one but you will never regret it!!!

Faye

MAX Transformation story #21

Faye, MAX Transformation story #21 – Before and After picture

> **"Beside the physical changes, I'm truly happier than I can ever remember being... EVER!!!"**
> *-Lee Pongracz*

Hi, I'm Lee and I'm a MAX -a-holic!!!

My story is like many of yours - I have been on the diet rollercoaster all my life... even managed to hit my "goal" weight a few times! :-) Graduate high school and prepare for college – go on a diet, 30th birthday arriving in a few months – go on a diet, get engaged – go on a diet, turning the dreaded 40... go on a diet!! Dizzy yet? ;-)

Then about 3 years ago I was diagnosed with Lupus. It took 11 different doctors, 3 university hospitals and 16 months of hell to figure out what was wrong with me. I'm much more fortunate than others as I only have 5 out of 11 markers so far. My worst 3 symptoms are hives, sporadic hair loss, and I now have a difficult time regulating my body temperature. After my diagnosis, I had to go back to UPENN every three months for blood work and biopsies, and I have been on countless topical and oral steroids, Enbrel, and Plaquenil. My primary doctor, Rheumatologist, and Dermatologist, all prepared me for what could (and most likely would) eventually happen to me as new systems progressed.

Then a year and a half ago I found MAX and it changed my life in more ways than I ever imagined possible. I am in the best shape of my life! Beside the physical changes, I'm truly happier than I can ever remember being... EVER!!! I have my doctors stumped because I have had no progression and no new symptoms, and I believe with all my heart it's because of MAX. A few months ago I went to a local doctor, recommended to me by UPENN, because I had developed some painful hives and my hair was falling out in clumps yet again, and I just knew they were going to put me back on steroids like they had done before. I was so upset and felt defeated. This new doctor reviewed my chart and asked me how I lost all the weight and how I was feeling, so I told her all about the MAX program. By the end of my visit she told me that if I could manage the pain from the hives and they don't get any worse, and I don't mind some hair loss, that she would not put me on anything for the time being. I was shocked and as soon as I walked out of that office – my first 2 text messages were to my husband, and then my MAX instructor – Scott Schneider!!

The program is amazing and the people are incredible!! They push me, make me laugh, and inspire me every single day.

I've had so many firsts on this journey - from finally losing weight the healthy way, to doing my first one minute plank, to running my first mile, then 5-k, then 10-mile... nope – that is not a typo my friends!! I still can't believe I did that craziness!!! :-)

I love my West Windsor family and I am so grateful to Scott Schneider and his family for the sacrifices they have made to change so many lives!

Lee Pongracz

MAX Transformation story #22

"**Every class I made it to was a victory.**"
-Rachel Warsaw

9/9/09 was supposed to be the day that changed my life forever, the day that I changed my destiny. It was supposed to be the beginning of my new healthy life. It was the day that I went under the knife and had gastric bypass surgery. At almost 300 lbs., I was never going to be that fat girl anymore. I was going to get healthy and stop this downward spiral I was on. But, like 75% of people who have bariatric surgery, the results did not last, and I was left as hopeless as ever about my ability to change. I am a fat girl who is destined to have progressively declining health like my dad, who at 60-something years old has more medical issues than seem humanly possible. My dad, who wants to live his life fully and enjoyably, but can't because he has so many limitations stemming for not caring for himself.

Fast forward to November 2012, when my son's karate school puts up a sign for a new fitness program; get healthy in 10 weeks! My husband (who's already thin) is intrigued. He signs up, and is member number 1 at the new East Windsor 10-Week-Fitness. My response: "another fad that isn't going to work for anyone in the long run". But it does, and I see him change- toning, strengthening, happier. I attend the first graduation with him, and I know this is not for me; all the clapping, high fives, and cheering were not what I needed or wanted. But that graduation did something, it inspired me to do something. I sought out other options, and adopted my new quest to be "Fit by 40." I tried a number of different things, and I failed everything I tried. 40 was getting closer and closer, and I knew that I was no closer to the goal of fitness. That hopelessness crept up, and I knew it was never going to happen for me. The only thing that gave me a glimmer of hope, was the MAX Secret Page. Seeing the results of others, and my husband's ongoing success helped me resign to the fact that maybe this was something that could work for me. Almost a year after my husband signed up, I knocked on the door of

Kate Finnegan and said "I think I am ready now." I signed up, taking each day at a time, every class I made it to be a victory. I was just waiting for the day that I would fall off track, and go back to my miserable self. But time passed, and I started enjoying class. I followed the nutrition to the best of my ability, and changes started happening. I felt physically better than I had my entire life. I started enjoying the high fives and the clapping. I made friends with people who have the same goals as me, and a little over a year later I feel great. I know a bad day can be made better by a good workout.

Oh there are ups and downs, and I am not perfect. I still have to challenge the demons in my head telling me eventually I will fail at this. But in the end, I know that my destiny has changed. MAX has given me the ability to live my life adventurously, unapologetically, and full of joy.

Rachel Warsaw

MAX Transformation story #23

Rachel Warsaw, MAX Transformation story #23 – After and Before picture

"I have seen the best results with The MAX Challenge's fitness and nutritional program."
-Prerna (Penny) Gupta

Since joining The MAX at Hamilton in September, I have seen myself having more energy in the afternoon. Before The MAX, around one o'clock in the afternoon, I would feel sluggish and want to take a nap. Now that I am exercising almost daily, I don't take naps and do not feel sleepy after work. I am motivated to workout daily and feel better about myself. The nutrition was the key for me and eliminating foods like dairy, potatoes, and sugary treats, my body has felt a lot better and I do not feel bloated.

I have learned new ways to cook healthier and with ingredients like coconut milk and adding more vegetables to my meals. I have stayed positive even when there were days I went off track. And when these days happened, I had instructors and friends help me get back on track. There is one great thing, the words I can't and giving up were never an option for me and everyone pushed me to go to the MAX. When working out, the instructors and other MAX ers', always made class fun and entertaining and always were positive!

Me personally, have done the gym, commercial weight loss programs and personal trainers; and I have seen the best results with The MAX Challenge's fitness and nutritional program. With this intense program, I have challenged myself to experiment new exercises such as performing a plank in push up position or a full sit up. These are exercises I could/ would not attempt because I was out of shape. Now, after the first ten weeks, I perform both and challenge myself to try new things the instructors, Heather, Noel and Michael throw at me!

I have meet amazing people and learned unique ways to conquer my obstacles with weight, exercise and nutrition. After each class, we would chat about new ways of preparing foods differently and attend events like the Color Me Rad. I always talk with members to stay motivated and seek new ideas form the web such as Pinterest.

My wedding was in November and everyone I saw said I looked great. Also, many asked how did I lose the weight and I replied I joined The MAX at Hamilton and never looked back!

Prerna (Penny) Gupta

MAX Transformation story #24

"The culture of The MAX Challenge has made me a better person in all aspects of my life."
-Brian Krutzel

It's hard to believe that it was only 7 months ago when I first joined The MAX Challenge. I wanted no part of it but my fiancé begged me to join. In truth, I was terrified to walk in the doors. I was obese, suffered from severe obstructive sleep apnea, and had digestive issues from Crohn's disease. My energy was at an all-time low and I never thought I would be able to keep up.

The first couple of weeks were challenging to the point that I was nauseous after class but they were so much fun that I kept coming back. The instructors and students were so friendly, encouraging, and support-ive. I was instantly hooked. A couple of weeks went by and I started noticing that I had a more energy (despite getting up at 5am every day for class).

Flash forward to today. I'm in the best shape of my life, my sleep apnea is gone, and my Crohn's symptoms have improved from the nu-trition. I've never had so much fun working out and cooking in my life. The MAX Challenge means the world to me and has turned my life around. The friends I've made are invaluable and have been a HUGE positive influence on me. Not just physically but also spiritually. The culture of The MAX Challenge has made me a better person in all as-pects of my life.

I look forward to class every single day and can't imagine my life with-out The MAX Challenge. Going to class is like brushing my teeth. I just do it! To anyone reading this that is thinking about taking the next step. Just walk in the doors. The MAX Challenge works!

Brian Krutzel

MAX Transformation story #25

Brian Krutzel, MAX Transformation story #25 – Before and After picture

> "For the first time in many years I could shop anywhere I wanted instead of the plus size department."
> -Theresa Marich

I have tried every diet and program known to man without lasting success but MAX has helped me to change my life. Before MAX, I was constantly tired, ate without thinking and I was very over weight. I didn't have the energy to get through my day and I felt like I wanted to go to sleep as soon as I came home from work. I didn't get any exercise and couldn't imagine how to start getting more active. I nervously joined MAX with a friend and we both thought we'd do this for 10 weeks and then we would be finished. After the first couple weeks, I made new friends and started to feel stronger and healthier. I was surprised to realize that I was able to do things in class that I couldn't do when I started and I had lost some weight. I began to think that I actually liked working out and I noticed how much better I felt when I ate healthier. I was amazed that a few weeks could make me feel so different. That was the beginning. I continued with MAX and eventually lost 60+ lbs. and multiple clothing sizes. For the first time in many years I could shop anywhere I wanted instead of the plus size department. My cholesterol improved so much that I was able to eliminate a cholesterol med that I had taken for over 10 years. In addition my blood pressure and sugar levels had changed dramatically. My own doctor didn't even recognize me in the waiting room when she passed by and was so surprised when she saw me in the exam room. She couldn't believe the changes that she saw and was planning to join MAX herself! I now have more fun with my husband and kids because I have more energy. I recently participated in a biometric screening at work. It is an exam that provides information about your risk for certain diseases and medical conditions and helps you to take actions to improve your health. In the past I have always stayed away from this screening because I knew my numbers were going to tell me that I needed to make changes. This year I decided to take the screening and passed 8 out of 9 categories and earned $300 toward my health spending account. I was so surprised that 8 months at MAX could have such amazing results. I can now enjoy the activities I used to watch. If feels so amazing to be a part of all the fun things going on around me. I'm happier, less stressed and I feel so much more confident. I look forward to each day and the challenges ahead. I continue to be amazed at how good I feel when I go to class and I make better choices about my food and activities. I am eating healthier so my family is also eating healthier and I see them opting for better choices on their own now. Several of my friends have joined MAX and they also look amazing and I can see them getting stronger and healthier. It truly is so great to see. I don't look at it as dieting and exercising. My nutrition is now a part of my lifestyle and I think of MAX as a place to go to be active in an environment that is positive and encouraging. No matter how tired I am when I walk in, I feel amazing when I walk out and the rest of my day is better. The instructors support you every step of the way with nutrition tips, encouragement and the right amount of push to help you achieve more than you ever thought possible. Your fellow MAX ers help you in class, out of class and through the MAX Facebook website. You can ask a question and have an answer in seconds. The support is amazing. I also recently started using the MAX App on my IPhone and I really like the convenience with my busy schedule. I love when I see a MAX Magnet on a car and think "oh yeah"! I can't thank the people at MAX enough and I continue to look forward to my journey of challenging myself and seeing what I can do. Take it to the MAX!

Theresa Marich

MAX Transformation story #26

> ### "I hated going to gyms. Just wasn't my thing. Now I don't want to miss a class."
> #### -Alison Cohen

Hi my name is Alison and I joined the MAX Challenge offered at SIUH. I'm just completing week 6 and I'm a new and improved me! Back in December after visiting with my physician my cholesterol levels and Thyroid function were awful. I was at my heaviest. I physically and mentally felt awful. In a matter of 6 weeks I've gone from a size 14 to a 10. Lost 9 inches and 8 lbs. although the numbers show the changes physically, I have changed mentally. I've embraced the nutrition and I'm eating better. I don't treat this as a diet but as a new way of eating. I plan meals ahead of time which has been an easy way to stay on track. I love the new friendships and camaraderie among my fellow MAXers. The MAX pages are a tremendous support system; they offer inspiration, sharing of recipes, questions and answers to clarify program, and overall a great resource and network.

Roseann Camarda and Toby have been great coaches and my biggest cheerleaders in this process. I've already signed up for the next challenge as I want to continue with this program.

I hated going to gyms. Just wasn't my thing. Now I don't want to miss a class. I enjoy the women in my class and the atmosphere is comfortable and fun and most importantly supportive.

I've been talking about the MAX challenge to friends and family and a few have signed up for future challenges!

I'm looking forward to shopping for a new wardrobe!

I can't say enough about the program and I hope more take advantage of the MAX.

Alison Cohen

MAX Transformation story #27

"Every day I went back, I felt more confident in myself and pushed myself a little harder each day."
- Jill Morales

My name is Jill Morales and I am 44 years old. I joined The MAX of Woodrow September 8, 2014. I was a size 16 going into an 18 in pants, and an extra-large in shirts, a size I hadn't been in years. I was disgusted and I had to do something.

Before I joined The MAX of Woodrow, I was a yo-yo dieter. You name it, I did it. From Isagenix, Medias, Body by Vi, to low carbs to no carbs, to Nutrisytem and Weight Watchers. Yes they did work, but as a temporary fix, and when I stopped the diet, I gained my weight back and then some. I didn't even feel so great physically on these diets.

I was always into exercising. I have a stack of workout DVD's I would use at home 2 or 3 days a week which bored me because I was alone. I had joined a few different gyms with my Husband and friends. Well needless to say, when they didn't go, I didn't go because I hated to work out alone. That's when friends started to tell me about The MAX of Woodrow. I "liked" the page on Facebook so I could follow and see what everyone was saying about it. I had a few friends and coworkers who joined, and they would tell me how much they loved it. I read peoples comments and there was never anything negative about it. I read about how much fun it was, how much they enjoyed it compared to other places they had gone, and how The MAX of Woodrow became their family. After hearing and reading all the positives about The MAX of Woodrow, I joined the 2nd challenge.

Everything I was told and that I read was the truth. In the beginning, I was nervous and very embarrassed when I couldn't do the exercises the same as everyone else was doing, and when I couldn't keep up with the pace or reps. My instructor Teressa and fellow MAXers assured me that in time I would be doing more reps and keeping up the pace. They encouraged me with every exercise to pace myself and not to try and keep up with the people around me. That made me feel so much more comfortable and a lot less embarrassed, and that is exactly what I did. Every day I went back, I felt more confident in myself and pushed myself a little harder each day. Again, my instructor and fellow MAXers were always encouraging and even noticed when I would do that extra push up or kept up with the jumping jacks. My MAX Family kept me motivated.

In the beginning of the challenge, I was weighing myself weekly. I would see a pound or more come off and then the scale would go back up. Feeling frustrated, I would talk to my MAX Family about it, and everyone said, "throw your scale away, you can tell your success by the way your clothes fit." I also had to keep in mind, muscle weighs more than fat. So with that being said, I have not been on the scale since September for that reason and for another. The other being I have an underactive thyroid, which I take 2 medications daily for. A person with a thyroid condition will lose weight a lot slower than the average person. I have come to terms with this, so I stay off the scale and use my clothes as my success guide. I suggest that to everyone in the MAX family. As of today, I am down to a size 12 and medium to large shirts.

Joining The MAX of Woodrow and having a "family" to workout with every day is an amazing feeling. I love that no matter what, there is always a "family member" to encourage me throughout our class. My eating habits are so much healthier, and I feel great! At times, I don't even look forward to my treat meal, because I feel so sluggish after I eat. Till this day, I have not missed a class. I am a MAX of Woodrow lifer!!! Thank you to Roseann for bringing The MAX to Staten Island!!

Jill Morales

MAX Transformation story #28

It took me trying to squeeze into a size 36 pant
to realize that something needed to be done.
- Mikki Curcio

Every member joins MAX with different goals in mind. While we both had goals of losing weight, we both experienced different "hidden" results. While they were not expected, they were simply incredible. In total, we lost close to 100 lbs. in a few short months.

Mikki: My goal of losing a few pounds was nothing out of the ordinary. However, what transpired over the next few years was something unexpected. I literally became a different person. While I did lose close to 50 pounds, so much more happened. I developed the self-confidence that I was missing and found a new, positive outlook on life.

Jimmy: I had been an athlete all my life. The key word is "had". I always leaned back on my high school sports days, which were over 10 years ago. It took me trying to squeeze into a size 36 pant to realize that something needed to be done. Well, 50 lbs. and 8 pant sizes later I was a new person. My most important result was realizing I had a FODMAP intolerance. My entire life I suffered from getting sick after I ate, and because of THE MAX's nutrition plan, I was able to determine what was causing it.

This is the impact we wish for everyone: to realize their potential and achieve their goals. With the support of our MAX family and instructors, this is possible for every member that steps on the mat. Our community of MAX ers is unlike any other. Nowhere else can we find a group of people, each with individual goals, coming together to help one another. For our instructors, it is personal. They give every bit of themselves to this program to ensure members achieve success.

For every high-five, for every "clap it up". For every first push-up and every "don't give up". This is MAX. This is who we are. We will never stop because frankly, we have forgotten how to.

Mikki Curcio

MAX Transformation story #29

Mikki Curcio, MAX Transformation story #29 – Before and After

> **"At 51 years old, I can honestly say, I am in the best shape of my life."**
> *- Dori Sabik*

As I think back to a cold day in November of 2014, my younger daughter Brittany calls me up and says Mom, I want to join MAX and would you like to join also. I tell her that's great for her but no I am not joining. A week or so passes and she then proceeds to tell me that she signed us up on Cyber Monday and our Challenge begins on January 12, 2015. I was more than touched when Brittany signed me up and paid for my challenge as my Mother's Day gift. I was a little apprehensive since I didn't know much about the program. I reached out to someone that I briefly knew to get some info on it. We learned that the nutrition plan consisted of no dairy which means no cheese or coffee cream and also no alcohol. I said how will I do that?

We began the challenge and completely embraced it. If we are doing this, we are doing it right or not doing it at all. We concentrated on the nutrition as equally as the workouts. We would food shop together and prep on Sundays, we would make MAX Compliant treats for our class. We searched clean eating recipes and were 100% compliant and never missed a workout and actually did several doubles as well. At 51 years old, I can honestly say, I am in the best shape of my life. I lost 18 pounds and Brittany 22 pounds in our first challenge. We don't miss the cheese and I surely don't miss the coffee cream. It is a true lifestyle change and we couldn't be happier or feel better. When you see results and feel amazing, you truly don't miss the foods that you thought you couldn't do without. As I always say, nothing tastes as good as being fit and trim feels. Brittany is so enthusiastic about the program and is always inspiring everyone in our class. She is also an instructor now and couldn't be happier. She is everyone's go to girl when they have nutrition questions.

We are on our 2nd challenge and we are just as excited for this challenge and MAX as day one. We absolutely love our workouts and love the healthy lifestyle we have become accustom to. Many friends and family members have recently joined MAX when they see our results and how passionate we are about our new lifestyle. MAX has truly brought joy and happiness to our lives and it makes us ecstatic to see our friends and family on their road to a healthier version of them. My older daughter Heather joined this second challenge and has completely rocked it. Her results to date are truly an inspiration to all. You will always find her motivating someone in class or giving them words of encouragement if they should need it. MAX gives you everything you need for a healthier lifestyle; you just need to follow the workouts and the nutrition. MAX helps you feel good and look even better. It truly improves your Mind, Body and Spirit. I am such a proud and lucky Mom to be able to embrace the MAX with both my daughters by my side. So what are you waiting for? Take it to the MAX …

Dori Sabik

MAX Transformation story #30

> ## "I was tired, unhealthy, unmotivated and unhappy with my body and my life."
> ### - Brittany Sabik

I n 2013, I started my fitness journey. I thought I could work out and eat whatever I wanted and lose the 15 to 20 pounds I needed to lose. It took me 6 months to lose 10 lbs. and I was ecstatic. Fast forward a year and a half later. I gained those 10 lbs. back and an extra 13 lbs. on top of them. I lost all motivation. I was tired, unhealthy, unmotivated and unhappy with my body and my life. I knew I needed to change. I had saw some of my friends were doing this MAX and I figured I'd ask them about it. They told me all about it and I thought this is perfect. This will reignite my passion for fitness and man was I right. I signed my mother and myself up for the January 12th 2015 challenge. That was the day my life changed forever. I started MAX and I ran with it. I utilized the tools given to me and I haven't looked back since. I am 24 lbs. down and have lost over 20 inches. Life is different now. I lead a MAX lifestyle and I am the happiest and healthiest I have ever been in the 24 years I have been living.

However the best part about my journey is not all the weight I have lost but how it has changed the lives of so many of my family members and friends who have joined after seeing my success. They are my true motivation to keep on taking it to the MAX every single day. I love this program, the members, and the instructors. I will be forever grateful for everything MAX has given me in life! And I am extremely honored that I get to pay it forward even more as an instructor that gets to lead people in their own fitness journeys. TAKE IT TO THE MAX!

Brittany Sabik

MAX Transformation story #31

In September 2013, my MAX journey began. I was ready to take charge of my health and change my life. In September 2011, I was diagnosed with male breast cancer. Many people don't realize it can happen to a man and most male breast cancer is undiagnosed or diagnosed too late. I underwent a mastectomy, chemotherapy, radiation and two reconstructive procedures, as well as other in-office treatments. After I was cleared by my doctors, I knew I needed to do something to change my eating habits and get healthy. Cancer is life changing. It is as if this was the wakeup call I needed.

I am employed as a bus driver, so most of my day is sedentary. I used to do charter trips all over the country; taking groups of people to different destinations and stopping at points of interest along the way. At every stop there is food involved, and not the healthy kind. Mostly it was fast-food and buffets. The days were long, so there was no time for exercise and I would get back to the hotels late at night, eating more unhealthy foods and snacks before going to sleep. The next day, I would grab a quick breakfast before heading out for the day and repeating the same process.

Prior to MAX, I would try and make smarter choices, I always ate vegetables; chose brown rice over white rice; actually preferred sweet potatoes over other potatoes and always ate grilled chicken. I've done Weight Watchers' in the past and learned how to eat healthier and make good choices but this was not enough. I needed to have a structured nutritional plan and I needed to be held accountable for my actions.

I saw the MAX billboard by my house but didn't really know about the program. I heard that it was expensive but at this point I was willing to try anything. I had a gym membership that I was paying monthly for, actually went a few times but then lost my way. I was paying for a gym membership that I wasn't even using, so what did I have to lose.

I called the MAX center in Edison and spoke to Jason Hoffman. I told him a little bit of my story and he told me to come in tomorrow to try a class. The next day I went to the class. I was warmly welcomed, met Jason in person, spoke to him about my situation and I did the class. I think it was a Thursday, so it was leg day and that is usually a tough class. I made it through the class and I knew there was something different about this program, something different about the people involved and I knew it was something that could help me. The nutrition plan was something that I felt I could handle. It was basic and not too confusing. I changed my milk for almond milk, I changed sugar to Stevia, got used to not having dairy, eating more vegetables and my fruit before noon. Before long it was just a way of life. I loved going to class and seeing the same people day in and day out and soon these people became friends and now my MAX family. If you don't show up to class, they look for you, they make sure you are okay and if you are having trouble or falling off, they help guide you back. A week and a half after I started my journey, my wife joined. We are both healthier and in better shape because of MAX. We recommend this program to everyone we can. With the help of MAX, I have lost a total of 90 pounds and have kept it off. I was a challenger winner in September 2014.

Robert Keenan

MAX Transformation story #32

Robert Keenan, MAX Transformation story #32 – Before and After picture

> **"Like many before me, I came in with diabetes, requiring various pills and a weekly injection I did myself."**
> *- Alan Burkholtz*

On my one year MAXiversary I feel great! Better than I have for a long time. The physical change is obvious, and started about 10-20 days into my first challenge, but the part you can't see has been miraculous. Like many before me, I came in with diabetes, requiring various pills and a weekly injection I did myself. (That was a challenge every Monday morning) I lost 20 lbs. and countless inches by the end of my first challenge, so I was able to stop the injections. And get out of bed in the morning without all the creaking and cracking in my knees and back. And I slept better. By the beginning of this year I was down another 20 lbs., more inches, and was told I could stop all my diabetes pills. All of them! (No Way! Yeah, Way!) And I was thrilled to be part of the Old Bridge MAX family and the entire MAX Nation. I wanted to pay back my MAX family and set some long range goals, even to eventually be an Instructor, so I started to coach in my 2nd challenge and then I became a MAX Certified Instructor earlier this year. Me! I still can't believe it's me in the mirror but I'm getting used to it. I've given away a ton of clothing and keep having to get smaller clothes about once a month or so. And I feel weird if I haven't worked out at least once a day. Me! Really! I can't believe those thoughts are even in my head. So if you have any excuse or reason for not starting MAX or for slowing down, inbox me, call me, stop me in the street, whatever, because I've probably overcome the same thing. I am wrapped up tight for every workout and 5K and have to modify here and there, but I do it! And I stick to the nutrition plan that has become a way of life. Thank God for MAX and all of you associated with it. I love you all.

Postscript: I just had my Second Year MAXiversary and I still go every day and I attend MAX Instructor training on Saturday mornings. I even teach two sections at MAX Instructor Boot camp. Yup, that's me. Former fat guy. Feeling great. Sure I've had some setbacks, but that's the great thing about MAX, it's so forgiving and motivating. Who wants to look back when the future is so bright? MAX On!

Alan Burkholtz

One Year MAXiversary – June 24, 2013 – 2014

MAX Transformation story #33

> *"I tried to live a positive life but how can you love others if you don't love yourself first."*
> *- Heather Sabik*

At 23 years old I was feeling at my lowest point in my life. I was tired, depressed, and not a happy person overall. In 2013, I decided I needed a change & I lost 50 pounds! 2 years later & I gained almost all my weight back. I was sad but I was more disappointed in myself. I worked hard & I felt like a total failure. Those feelings of depression & sadness filled my life once again. I was not going to let myself feel that low so I knew I needed to change. My sister & my mom joined The MAX in the beginning of 2015. They were my inspiration to really get back into the swing of things & lose this weight. They bought me my MAX Challenge for an early birthday gift and man was I excited. I could not have asked for a better gift. I had no doubt in my mind that I would seriously rock my first challenge. March 29th, 2015 is when my life changed completely but at the time I didn't realize that. I stood in the back of class, quiet as can be. I HATED the mirrors. I didn't even want to look at myself because this feeling of disgust came across me. What a horrible feeling knowing I didn't like my body or even want to see myself working out. I tried to live a positive life but how can you love others if you don't love yourself first. After my first day I went home, I studied my booklet, wrote notes & just kept saying to myself I GOT THIS! I talked to myself daily & reminded myself that I can do anything I put my mind too. I weighed in & took my measurements and I said to myself, HEATHER- you are NOT allowed to step on this scale or take your measurements until week 10 is FINISHED! I didn't want numbers to cloud my brain & get in my head. I didn't want any distractions; my mind was on the prize. During the 10 weeks, I focused on how I felt, learned about nutrition, my mood was more positive, and I was overall a happier person. I even forgot about my weight because of how amazing I truly felt. Forgetting the numbers & just focusing on myself & this new journey I was on really made me love my body. In class, I now have to stand up in the front by the mirrors because I love looking at myself! The confidence I have gained is what amazes me the most. I am a different person not only physically but also mentally. Besides my nutrition & workouts, my attitude has improved. My family & friends have said how much I have embraced a positive outlook on everything in life. The MAX has seriously changed my entire world around. I lost 31 pounds and 15 ½ inches during my first challenge

Heather Sabik

MAX Transformation story #34

So here is my success story.

A friend of mine belongs to MAX of Old Bridge and was telling me about this fitness class he was taking and he said was working awesome, he lost a ton of weight and feels and looks awesome. So I decided to check it out and saw that there was a location opening not far from my house in the near future. I started emailing Stephanie from MAX of Toms River to get more information about the whole process and we went back and forth a ton of times, and I always had an excuse as to why I shouldn't join. You see, this wouldn't be the first time I have signed up for something like this, I have worked with personal trainers, exercise videos, weight watchers...you name it, I tried it. Eventually I gave in and decided to sign up for the 10 week challenge as a onetime thing to kind of get myself back into the swing of things with working out and eating right.

So a few weeks passed before the kick off and grand opening. I remember sitting there listening to Bryan Klein talking about changing the world 1 person at a time and I thought this guy was nuts, but I sat through it and took it all in. That night I was prepping food and getting ready for my first week. That Monday was my first time working out in years and I was not pleased with where I was with my fitness level, but I gave it my all. The next day wasn't much easier, but I kept coming back and giving it everything I had. Each class I was able to do less and less modified exercises till I was able to get through a whole class without doing any. I didn't realize it at the time but I was doing exactly what that crazy guy Bryan was talking about, I was showing up every day and giving it my all.

I continued for the next 10 weeks to give it my all and tried to stick to the nutrition as best I could and at the end of the 10 weeks, I was shocked when I got a call from Stephanie making sure I was coming to the end of challenge celebration because I was a finalist!!! I was kind of shocked since I did not see the transformation that everyone else saw. When I was called up and Stephanie began telling everyone a little bit about me, she said something that has stuck with me since, that she could tell right away that I "got it". I understood what it would take for this program to work. And I did, I realized that I was only get to get out of this program what I put it, and I wanted to change. That night I won the prize for Biggest Transformation and I couldn't have been happier, all of the work I was putting in paid off.

That was over a year ago now and I have completed 5 challenges and have even become a coach, helping other people achieve their goals in this program as well. But that's not all, I have become a happier, healthier and ways more confident person. I am doing things that I never in a million years I would be able to do. I have run in 3 mud runs and I am signed up for a Tough Mudder. I enjoy working out now and when I get boarded I go for runs. The old me would have never gone for a run unless my house was on fire. What this program has given me can't be measured, but it can a little bit. I am down over 100lbs and countless inches and couldn't be happier. The old unhappy me no longer exists and the new happy and healthy me can't wait to see what the next 12 months will bring...

Matthew Sutera

MAX Transformation story #35

> *"The first comforting thing I saw as I walked through the door, was that there were people of all sizes in my class."*
> *- Teresa Tollevsen*

My name is Teresa Tollevsen and I joined the MAX of Hazlet when it opened on September 29th 2014. I've had a weight problem my entire life, and probably at my lowest weight I was wearing size 12's highest weight size 20's. After having children I would lose and gain weight over and over again doing Weight Watchers, Nutra System, South Beach Diet, 17 Day Diet (I think I tried them all). Then after hitting my 40's and going through bouts of depression and anxiety I hit my highest weight ever. When I saw posts about the MAX in Hazlet on Facebook I decided to look into it, and after a lengthy conversation with Marc Naparstek, the owner, I decided to join. Unfortunately the center wasn't opening for a few more weeks, so I had plenty of time to be nervous about it and wonder what I got myself into.

The morning of my first class I was so nervous. My stomach was doing flip flops, and I thought I'd throw up. I was so worried I'd pass out from doing the workout since I was so out of shape. The first comforting thing I saw as I walked through the door, was that there were people of all sizes in my class. Men and women, young and old, seemingly fit, and completely out of shape. In the first time in my life I didn't feel intimidated about being in a gym. Well, needless to say I made it through my first class, then my first week, then my first challenge. As the weeks went on I was getting stronger and stronger, being able to do things I couldn't do in the beginning. Holding planks for over a minute, doing a full burpee, increasing my weights, squatting and lunging lower. It all started to fall into place and somewhere in my third challenge I became addicted. I hated to miss a class, I started going to the gym on business trips (before the MAX I would pack gym clothes, but never take them out of the suitcase), and I started running. Running was something I could never do, not even as a teenager, and my first time out I ran a mile which was more than I could do as a 16 year old kid in gym class. My confidence level went through the roof, I started to think there was nothing I couldn't accomplish.

Right now I am in my 4th challenge, I still haven't reached my goal, but with the MAX it is the first time in years that I know I will reach it. I am at the point that I'm hitting a lot of plateaus, but I've put away the scale to not get discouraged. I'm definitely still losing inches so I just keep going to my class, and following the nutrition. We were asked to fill out a goal card one of the first weeks that we started. They asked for a long term goal and I remember writing "I want to finish this". So many times in the past I would lose weight, hit a plateau, get frustrated and go back to my normal eating habits. This of course would cause me to gain the weight back, and then some. With the MAX I will never go back to my old habits. The nutrition is easy to follow, I've discovered so many new foods that are delicious, and I never feel deprived with my treat meal. I honestly love the workouts and cannot imagine my life without the MAX.

The reason this program works is the nutrition has alternatives for everything, and most of the alternatives are really tasty. The staff, and trainers are awesome, they know you by name, and are so encouraging and helpful. The MAX family is the biggest support system I have ever been a part of. The Facebook page is so informational and supportive. The people in the class you attend become some of your biggest motivators and challenge you to your fullest. And what other gym reaches out to you when you miss too many classes. I truly think the reason I love the MAX the most is because you go to class, do what the trainer tells you to do, sweat up a storm, and go home feeling awesome every day!!

Thank you to the MAX family of Hazlet, NJ, and Bryan Klein for changing my life!!

Teresa Tollevsen

MAX Transformation story #36

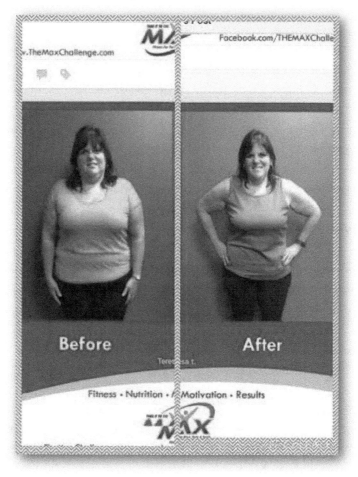

Teresa Tollevsen, MAX Transformation story #36 – Before and After picture

"I loved going there every day to see my favorite instructors and friends, I stayed compliant because it was "only 10 weeks""
- Carly Irizarry

My name is, I started The MAX Challenge on March 31st, 2014 in Old Bridge, NJ and am currently down 90lbs!

I was a store manager for a retailer at the time that I heard about MAX. I was the heaviest I've ever been at over 250lbs (and just 27 years old) when a woman came in and said - and I will never forget this - "I need some help, I went from a size 14 to a size 6 and I have no idea what fits me anymore". I had to ask her what she did to lose the weight and she said "Why, MAX of course!"

At the time I heard about the program I wasn't in the right mind frame to lose weight. I had tried EVERYTHING and I mean everything to lose weight. Weight watchers, Jenny Craig, Accuweight, 4 different gyms, and even sat in a seminar to get weight loss surgery - nothing worked and the surgery scared me too much. I thought I would be this heavy for my entire life - and then I walked into the Old Bridge, NJ location.

MAX easily became my respite. I loved going there every day to see my favorite instructors and friends, I stayed compliant because it was "only 10 weeks" and really pushed myself. In those 10 weeks I didn't miss a single class, I ate right, made friends that would last a lifetime, and lost over 40lbs in just my first challenge. I felt like a whole new me! It was the little things that I noticed first - the ability to bring groceries up 3 flights of stairs and not get winded, my pants getting looser, and my ability to hold a plank! Each milestone I hit was celebrated through my MAX friends, instructors, and the Facebook group. My transformation pictures started getting over 300 likes, people reached out to me for help - it really changed my whole perspective of my weight loss journey. It gave me a sense of accountability I never had before.

It is now almost 5 challenges later and quickly approaching my one year MAXiversary. In that year, I have lost 90lbs, have gone from a size 20 to a size 6 pant, have gotten my fiancé addicted to the program (who in his first challenge lost over 30lbs), and see this as something I will cherish and continue to do for the rest of my life.

I can't say thank you enough for this amazing program. It took me 28 years to be proud of myself and have a positive self-image and that is something you can only find with the MAX Challenge.

Carly Irizarry

MAX Transformation story #37

'The MAX Challenge has saved my life in more ways than I could ever imagine possible."
- Kathy Lawlor

There was never one particular reason for my physical and mental deterioration, but a series of unfortunate life events that occurred one after the other, collectively wreaking havoc on my well-being. Prior to giving birth to my son in 2005, I was in the best shape of my life. An avid runner, I had pushed my mile pace down to a 7 and a half minute mile and had never felt better with my training. After he was born, I had a very difficult time losing the pregnancy weight and as a result, became very discouraged. I was bombarded with various stresses afterwards and found that I had little to no motivation outside of work and motherhood; they both completely consumed me. In June 2010, I suffered a severe back injury. During the next couple of years of grappling with physical therapy and dealing with the insurance company, more weight piled on.

I have tried countless ways to lose the weight and get back in shape, but all of them required little to no effort on my part. They were all those quick fixes you see in advertisements; weight loss centers, homeopathic remedies, and gyms. After my back healed, I finally found the courage to try a boot camp. The exercises were at such a high level that I eventually was sidelined once again with back issues. I was completely discouraged and beginning to accept that this is how my life would be.

After spending another couple of years allowing my back to heal, I received a postcard in the mail for The MAX Challenge. My first reaction was that this was just another gimmick at which I would miserably fail just like all other past attempts. My second thought was that I really did not want to risk another back injury. So I ripped up the post card and threw it away. A few months later, another post card showed up and without hesitation, I ripped that one up too. A couple of months later, a well-timed post card showed up just around New Year's Day. This time I let it peak my interest.

I had just turned 50 a few months earlier and promised myself that I would try my best to succeed at losing some weight over the course of the year. It was also New Year's resolution time. I sent an inquiry online and received an immediate response from one of the owners of the center. Within a day or two of our first contact, we arranged to speak so that all of my questions could be answered. Lisa spent more than 45 minutes on the phone with me providing every detail of the program. I was so impressed with the time she invested in me not knowing whether or not I would join. After a couple days of consideration, I skeptically signed on and started my first challenge on January 12, 2015.

The MAX Challenge has saved my life in more ways than I could ever imagine possible. Unlike any other program out there, this one absolutely resonated with me. The sense of community, incredible support network, easy to follow nutrition, and classes are all contributing factors to its success. My back issues have not returned thanks to the phenomenal MAX instructors who are always cognizant of individual needs. I am so blessed to share this incredible journey with my fellow MAX ers. These wonderful people who I didn't know six months ago have played a huge role in my success and I hope I've had the same impact on them. I love starting my day with them!

In six months, I've lost 37 pounds and 4 sizes. I never imagined that at 50 years old I would be saying, "These size 6 pants are getting loose." I am so thankful that I didn't rip up that third post card. Take it to the MAX!

Kathy Lawlor

MAX Transformation story #38

> ## "I wanted and needed to change but didn't know what to do."
> ## - *Rosalind Davis*

I was out having dinner with my girlfriend in January 2015 when I mentioned that I was in the process of planning my son's birthday party. My girlfriend said why are you planning him a party you should be planning yourself a 50th birthday party. She was downright adamant that I have this party. After leaving dinner I felt bad about a lot of things and began to reflect on what I had accomplished and had yet to achieve. One thing that bothered me the most was my weight. I was too tired, depressed, aching knees and back, taking 2 high blood pressure medications and just being very unhappy with myself at this point. I wanted and needed to change but didn't know what to do. You see I had already tried every diet and weight loss program known to man, but the weight came off for a period of time then back it came with a vengeance.

On FB I kept getting these ads about The MAX and come take a trial class. This caught my attention so I got up enough nerve to take the trial class. Surprising I made it through without passing out. They announced there was going to be a raffle and all those taking the trial class were entered. As I waited my turn to choose from the bowl I said to myself I'll do the 10 weeks if I get 50% of membership. When it was my turn I chose the 50% off the membership. I just looked up to the ceiling and said ok looks like I'm in. I decided to forgo my birthday party and took some of my money and paid for my 10 week challenge.

On January 28, 2015 in my 6am class my trainer acknowledged my birthday along with the class. I was overwhelmed that I just cannot describe my emotions. I continued for the next ten weeks and I went from 2 medications down to one and currently working on no medications. When I started the class I was wearing 3X pants and shirts, now I'm wearing an XL. My depression gone, back and knee pain minimum to none, and so much more energy for myself and family. The major component that this lifestyle has given me back is my confidence. It was hidden under all of my other issues but now it has been awakened. No longer do I look to food as comfort but it's to sustain my body,

I owe my new life to The MAX.

I am eternally grateful for this program.

Rosalind Davis

MAX Transformation story #39

> **"Not only was I letting myself down, but I wasn't being the wife or mother I always wanted to be."**
> *- Meghan Campbell*

Hi!! My MAX journey started at the Hazlet, NJ location January 12, 2015, all thanks to a friend who kept bragging about the program.

As a mother of a 4yr & 1.5yr old, wife to police officer who works impossible hours, and I also work as a part time night shift ICU nurse, I could a book of excuses and rationalization as to why I don't have time to work out or eat healthy!! Most moms tend to put ourselves at the end of the priority list every day. I had been unhappy with my appearance and post-kids body shape for quite a while, but my rock bottom was a combination of my life insurance premium rising, my size 18 pants screaming when I buttoned them, and having absolutely no sexual desires what so ever. Not only was I letting myself down, but I wasn't being the wife or mother I always wanted to be. I realized the only way I could get to a MAX class was if I snuck out of the house at 0430 to go to the 5am class, and be home before anyone woke up.

I took that first challenge like my life depended on it - because it did!! At the end, I may have lost 30lbs but I gained so much more!! To date, I am halfway through my 3rd challenge and down 52lbs!!!

The 2 biggest reasons the MAX Challenge has worked for me over all previous diets, workouts, etc. I've tried are these: focus on goals and the support via Facebook & group classes. Face it, these days we are all constantly checking social media. I must subconsciously check Facebook 100times/day and every time I am reading posts from other MAX ers about their struggles, their triumphs, and their recipes. I feel connected and supported 24/7!!! The other successful tool for me has been setting goals, both short term and long. To keep a constant goal in mind, take small steps towards it every meal, every workout, every day and then to see myself CRUSH my goals is SO empowering!!! I started off with wanting to do 10 "big girl" (off my knees) push-ups, now I can do 20; I wanted to run a 5k. Started by running 2miles, now I can do a hilly 3.2 AFTER my MAX class!! I wanted to be at pre-baby weight, I'm 16lbs below that!

I still struggle with the nutrition and probably always will, but I know if I own up to it, let it go and recommit to being compliant I'll be ok. I can fall 1000 times as long as I get up 1001! I love who I am for my kids, for my husband, but mostly for ME!!!

Meghan Campbell

MAX Transformation story #40

> **"I was at a point where I was going to just accept where I was."**
> *- Joyce Mangino*

I started my MAX journey in January of 2014. Prior to joining I had been on again, off again with fitness. I was a lifetime member of a "diet program" that always worked for me, but yet it was truly a yo-yo experience. I would lose weight, but then get sidetracked only to gain back what I lost plus another ten pounds. For five years I had restarted going to weekly meetings and going to the gym and doing what always worked only to be met with absolutely no results and total frustration.

I would see pop up ads for MAX on my Facebook page. So I checked out the website. No, I don't think that's for me. I'm not an athlete! So fast forward about six months, one of my friends posted a "like" for the MAX of Princeton. She was a trainer at the gym I was going to. I asked her, "Do you have something to do with this?" She did! So I signed up!

I was, at that point, desperate. I was in my mid-fifties. I was overweight. I was frustrated and extremely unhappy. Nothing was taking the weight off. My shoulders ached. The range of motion in my joints was not good. I was stiff. I had written off my metabolism as dead and gone. I was at a point where I was going to just accept where I was.

So out the door I went to the kickoff, slipped on a patch of ice and landed on my tail bone. Determined to try this thing out, I got in the car and went. It's amazing what you can do when you dig deep. The winter of 2014 was a very cold one. I started classes in the morning, but then had a change of employment and needed to switch to the evening. 9:15 PM was our start time! I was determined to do this. When I would usually be dozing off on the couch watching television after a day's work, I was getting in my car and going to class. Most nights it was about 10 degrees out. I remember one night as we were leaving, someone announcing, "Hey, everybody, its nine degrees!" I even needed to open the car window on my way home from being so hot.

We were given a goal sheet to fill out. It had written on it: My Goal Is: I wrote down, "To lose 25 pounds." Then it said: My Target Date Is: I wrote down, "12/31/14." (One year later.) At the end of the first challenge I had lost 16 pounds! I never would have expected that! In total, I'm down 40 pounds. My metabolism did wake up!

It just feels so good to be comfortable in my own skin and to have the confidence that I've gained from MAX. My shoulders don't ache any longer. They are strong. I'm not stiff, and my range of motion is back to where it should be.

I've met some wonderful people. It's a great thing when you're in a room with others working to achieve the same goals. The motivation and support is beautiful.

You have to believe in yourself. You have to give yourself a chance. You have to love yourself.

Joyce Mangino

MAX Transformation story #41

Joyce Mangino, MAX Transformation story #41 – Before and After picture

> **"I am forever grateful and in debt for the blood, sweat and tears that have been shed from me."**
> *- Don Bolton*

My name is Don Bolton. I have been a MAX er since I walked through the doors of MAX of Shrewsbury on June 2nd 2014. I am currently 44 years old and at 43 I was 305 lbs. and on cholesterol and high blood pressure medication. My levels were completely out of control and I was in need of a life change.

I began my journey to a healthier me and decided to not look back but only forward. In my first 10 weeks I learned how to eat and to exercise like no other time in my life. I made all kinds of new and supportive friends. Needless to say I dove into this program and in my first 10 weeks I lost 45 lbs. and won my first challenge. In the following weeks I continued to work hard and lose more pounds but grow mentally and physically stronger every day. I went onto hit the 100 lb. weight loss in match of 2015. I have run 8 5k runs ... 3, 5 mike runs, 1 10k and most recently in April I ran a half marathon in under 2 hours. I currently sit at minus 112 lbs. and am not looking back at the old me and when I do I shake my head and say what were you thinking? Thank you MAX nation for the new lease on life you have given me. I am forever grateful and in debt for the blood, sweat and tears that have been shed from me.

Don Bolton

MAX Transformation story 42

> ### "I couldn't stand being in pictures and finding things to wear became painful and embarrassing."
> ### *- Kim Shafer*

I was always pretty much a thin person my entire life. During and after college I was into aerobics and was fit and thin. After having my children, twins included with a 75 pound weight gain, I found myself overweight inactive and totally unhealthy. I also quit smoking which added to my weight gain. Five years ago I was diagnosed with hypothyroidism, this also contributed to my weight gain. I couldn't stand being in pictures and finding things to wear became painful and embarrassing. I often shied away from seeing old friends that knew me when I was thin. I was depressed about my weight but put on a happy face and laughed it off while inside I was crying. I tried so many things from diet pills, shakes, work out videos and nothing worked. I weighed as much as my husband...that was really embarrassing and I knew I had to do something but was as a loss as to where to turn. A good friend asked me to come to the MAX kick off with her and I resisted at first but finally gave in and went with her having no clue what to expect. I wasn't planning on joining...but after the meeting I decided to take the plunge with her and we both signed up for our first challenge. We have been MAX buddies ever since, going together most days and supporting each other....I can't say enough how that has really been extremely beneficial to us both. I guess you could say I figured I would fail again so I didn't take the before picture with MAX, this is my own picture. I think my success is based on the fact that I took it one day at a time, tried to focus on daily MAX workouts and follow the nutrition plan. One day turned one week and that turned into one challenge and after feeling fantastic while losing weight I have never looked back. I have lost a total of 80 pounds since joining The MAX of Old Bridge In June of 2014. Now, buying clothing that is five sizes smaller is fun and exciting. I love taking pictures and actually marvel at how far I have come. I am in the best shape of my life. My three kids are so proud of me as is my husband...he feels like a newlywed...23 years later! I have to add that he never once judged me for gaining all that weight, always made me feel beautiful and loved me unconditionally. I did this for me but I cannot say how proud of me he is and happy that I am healthier. To be honest, getting ready to turn 50 has made me realize it's not all about how I look but about how my insides look and will help me live longer to be around for the people I love. Losing my own mother when she was only 56 years old has made me realize health is nothing to take for granted. I am also very proud of the changes my family has made in their nutrition and exercise choices...this has been a win win for me and my family and for that I am truly thankful. I am a perfect example of how you can lead a horse to water but you cannot make them drink. I had to wait until it was the right time for me to make the changes necessary to live a healthier lifestyle. I laugh at the naysayers that think MAX is a cult or it's not possible to keep it up...whatever other negative things anyone could ever say to me make me smile because I know the truth and so do all of the other MAX ers... we are the ones in the know and for that I am eternally thankful and appreciative....clap it up!

Kim Shafer

MAX Transformation story #43

Kim Shafer, MAX Transformation story #43 – Before and After picture

> *"I had no idea what to expect and hoped it would not be the beginning of just another failed attempt to lose weight and get healthy."*
> *- Allison Casais*

My story...

I began my MAX journey on March 24, 2015. It was the scariest and most exciting day all rolled in one. I had no idea what to expect and hoped it would not be the beginning of just another failed attempt to lose weight and get healthy. As I continued my journey, I realized that MAX Challenge worked and was something I could actually do successfully. Over the past four months, I have lost weight, and gained strength and confidence. Despite the fact that I have rheumatoid arthritis, making exercise more difficult and painful, I am able to make it through each exercise class as a result of the instructors and members who are always so supportive and encouraging. Also, after being on blood pressure medication for over 8 years, my dose was recently cut in half and the plan is to eventually wean myself off of it altogether. I have a long way to go, but I am headed in the right direction. My health and life is improving, and I thank the support of MAX Challenge as well as my friends and family for their constant support. It's not always easy, but it is always worth it.

Allison Casais

MAX Transformation story #44

"The support system at MAX is not like any other, always staff and members available.'
- *Nina Fersko-Gross*

You wouldn't think that I had so much energy at 54 years-old than I did ten years ago, but it's true!

I have struggled with many nutrition and exercise plans that had exhausted me; instead this new lifestyle the last six months not only helps me stay physically fit but it compliments my busy work and family life. A 45 minute workout is easy for anyone to fit into a 24 hour day. The nutrition plan is easy by keeping it simple by only planning two days at time so I'm not overwhelmed and I look forward to my treat meal every Saturday night. The support system at MAX is not like any other, always staff and members available. I don't get on the scale anymore but use the mirror and wonderful compliments from clients, coworkers, family and friends. This past birthday I definitely felt younger than last year.

Nina Fersko-Gross

MAX Transformation story #45

Nina Fersko-Gross, MAX Transformation story #45,
Before and After picture

"I have never done a workout like this in my life."
- Dawn Romano

Health is something I always wanted to achieve but didn't have the right tools to get me there. That is until I had a friend mention MAX. He told me how this could be a way to love exercise, get healthy and just feel better about myself. I've been over weight my whole life, and I needed to get off medications for high blood pressure and cholesterol. I always tried to lose weight the wrong way, from fad diets to diet pills nothing seemed to be right for me and my body. I thought it was hopeless to try a new program when everything else failed. When I mentioned the program to my daughter she had us signed up for the spring challenge2015 in a matter of minutes. We would take on this journey together, mother and daughter side by side encouraging each other the whole way. We used each other as an excuse not to miss a class; I would have to go if she was going. There was no backing out.

Following the nutrition, drinking plenty of water and working out five days a week was the perfect combination to start seeing the pounds melt off. I have never done a workout like this in my life. I have never done a push up or mountain climber or held a plank for that matter. It was challenging and I used all the modifications, but nothing was going to stop me and I was going to give it all I had for the full 10weeks. The first time walking in the Howell location I was nervous and thought I was going to be sick just thinking about working out in front of other people. This is why I never really liked going to the gym. That first day meeting the owners and trainers was great; everyone was so nice, warm and welcoming. I felt comfortable being there and at the end of the first class I was hooked. Working out was actually fun and I learned so much about fitness and myself. With everyone cheering me on in my weight loss it was a great experience that I will never forget. It lead me to win the spring challenge and lost over 30 pounds and gained confidence that I never had before. I owe my life to MAX of Howell for helping me get healthy and live a better life, with fewer pills. I can't thank them enough.

Dawn Romano

MAX Transformation story #46

"If you are willing to commit to the program and do the work, the program will work for you."
- Barry Bergman

My name is Barry Bergman and I'm a member of the Howell, NJ Center. I'd like to share how the MAX Challenge program has changed my life. First, let me tell you something about myself. I'm over 70 years old and was in terrible shape before I participated in my first Challenge. From a "structural" perspective, I have an artificial left hip joint and artificial left shoulder joint, bad knees, and had major abdominal surgery. So, you could say that I probably had a very small chance of success with the program.

As I write this on August 3rd, I've been a member since January 6th and I'm in the middle of my 3rd challenge. To date, I've lost 45 pounds, over 8 inches from my waist, 4 pants sizes, and feel better than I've felt since my 30's. My doctors...family and friends... are amazed with my results. If you are willing to commit to the program and do the work, the program will work for you.

When I started my first challenge, my first instructor, Elisa, worked closely with me and taught me modifications for every exercise routine. It wasn't until week 9 of the first challenge that I was able to go through a complete workout without modification. It wasn't until week 6 or 7 that I was able to do a full one minute plank. I'm now in the middle of my third challenge and fully expect that I'll be participating in the program for the rest of my life.

What makes the MAX Challenge program really different for me is the multi-phased approach of the program. The program is a combination of nutritional guidance, a well-balanced fitness program, and most important...strong motivation. The motivation not only comes from the instructional team, but motivation from fellow students. The class feels more like a family working together toward a common goal. My fellow students help me, cheer me on, and make me want to work harder. I can't say enough about the program...its' proven...it works.

Barry Bergman

MAX Transformation story #47

"I would NEVER have been that guy in the front of the room, clapping and yelling it up for others, high fiving anyone who comes within three feet of me."
- Steve Passmore

Thought I would toss my story in the mix for the MAX success stories. I attend the 6:00am class at the Bedminster location, and have been a member since it's opening in January 2015. I began my first challenge on January 12th. In the fall of last year, I noticed my co-worker started to look very lean and I asked what diet program he was using. He told me he was doing The MAX Challenge, which was new to me. He explained the program, and then over the next few weeks told me about his workouts and how the nutrition part of the MAX worked as well. I was pretty disgusted with my weight (280 lbs.! The most I'd ever weighed) as well as my less than perfect health overall (high blood pressure, sleep apnea, etc. etc.) I was told that a MAX location was opening in my area and they were just trying to find space. I found out in November that the new MAX location was opening in Bedminster....imagine my luck only 4 miles from home! I registered for the January class sight unseen...before ever meeting an owner or instructor, and weeks before they even held a sample class! I knew I had to try this and give it my all....

That first week in January of my first challenge is one I will never forget. Pitch dark outside and below zero temps as I drove to class. I get to my spot on the mat, and I could barely catch my breath during the workouts, my knees ached, my back hurt, legs, etc. etc. We've all been there! I just kept staring up at those before and after photos on the wall, thinking "I can do this...one more jumping jack, one more robot, one more burpee, I can do this"! Fast forward to March, the end of Bedminster's inaugural Challenge #1, and now we get to vote for the 5am/6am/7am/9:15am/8:30pm classmates who we believe have made the most progress, not only with weight loss, but participation, hard work/determination, a class leader, etc. Out of all those hard working members, I won! To think, my peers who work and struggle just as hard (some harder) as me, thought enough of me and my journey to vote for me as the winner of Bedminster's first ever Challenge. The surprise and appreciation I felt cannot be put into words. I vowed to make them all proud, cheer every last one on each morning, and show them I can so do this!!

I am happy to report I am currently in week 6 of my THIRD challenge! I try not to look at the scale very often, but last glance I am down 50lbs and my pant size has gone from 44/45 waist to 38. I am no longer taking two medications for high blood pressure, oh...and those knees don't ache nearly as much as they did in January. I can honestly say, this is the healthiest and best physical shape I have ever felt in my life. One thing I don't think anyone is aware of when they join The MAX, a hidden bonus you might say, which is all the self-esteem and confidence that you gain. I would NEVER have been that guy in the front of the room, clapping and yelling it up for others, high fiving anyone who comes within three feet of me. Not because I'm rude or stand off-ish, but because I wasn't happy with myself and ashamed/shy to put myself out there. Well no more, not this MAX er! I cannot thank my co-worker enough for sharing his MAX story with me last year, and to our instructors, owners, and most importantly all my new friends at the Bedminster MAX that make it so easy to want to get up at 5:00am and jump around on a mat....and LOVE every minute of it!

TAKE IT TO THE MAX!!!!!

Steve Passmore

MAX Transformation story #48

Steve Passmore, MAX Transformation story #48 – Before and After picture

> 'As my confidence soared, my life
> improved dramatically."
> - *Jenny DeSantis*

I had heard about something called The MAX Challenge opening in my neighborhood. I was very curious, however, sure that it would be another fad that would not work for me. My manager at work had won a gift basket that contained a gift card for the MAX for 1 challenge. As she joined and the weight fell off, I became intrigued. I grabbed a great Black Friday deal on my first challenge and started the MAX Challenge January 12, 2015. It was the best decision I have ever made. Sure the weight came off, inches were dropped, but I had no idea of the impact MAX would have on the rest of me. As my confidence soared, my life improved dramatically. My marriage and relationships with family and friends improved. I became so happy on the inside that it now radiates through my smile. MAX changed everything in ways I never thought possible. It changed my life and I am forever grateful. I tell everyone I can about MAX, and I share my before pics and motivational tips to keep people going forward. MAX has become my major focus, and I see now why is it called a "lifestyle" change. Everything changed and I can't see it ever going back to how it was before. I went to Vegas in July and ate like I never had before- salads, water, as healthy as I could. This was because I CHOSE to. Not because I felt I HAD to. That is the difference between a lifestyle change and a diet. MAX is an ongoing, living, breathing entity. It isn't a quick fix or a 10 week fast where you transform into a supermodel overnight. You get out every drop of sweat and muscle ache you put in. And I wouldn't change that for anything. Thank You MAX. Thank you Bryan Klein. Thank you too all my instructors and peers that push me.

Jenny DeSantis

MAX Transformation story #49

> ## "I can keep up with my kids and sometimes find myself with more energy than them."
> ### *- Amy Potpinka*

When I was young, I never had to watch what I ate. I could eat anything and not gain an ounce. I was very active. I played softball, basketball, and I was a cheerleader so I was always on the move. I never really learned to eat a proper diet, and I NEVER exercised outside of sports practice. Then, came college and along with that…the dreaded freshman 15. But I started college in a size 3 so I ignored the 15 pounds. During college I met my now husband. We would have such a great time together and I knew he loved me no matter what my size was, so I turned the other way as I bought bigger pants. Then came my two beautiful children. With my first born, I gained 50 pounds during that pregnancy. I lost most of it after he was born, but then I was too busy being a mom to make healthy meals and working out a priority for myself. With my second child I gained significantly less weight, however this time I never lost it. So, here I was 29 years old, and MANY pounds heavier. I was tired a lot, had low energy and besides taking care of my kids I was lazy. My moment of clarity came when I went to buy a pair of jeans and realized that I had somehow gone from a size 3 to a size 15! How did that happen?? Why did no one tell me!? Then I remembered a while back my sister was telling us about this fitness program she had found and showing us her baggy pants. At first, I thought I didn't have time to go the gym. I HATE going to the gym. But then she told me more about MAX and how it isn't like going to the gym. It sounded interesting and I said I'd like to try it, but never perused it. Now it's the holiday season and I'm beating myself up over all the holiday pictures that I don't like of myself. Right after New Year's, my sister sends me a link on Facebook to enter a drawing to win a free 10 week challenge. I said, ok, I'll fill it out and if I win I'll do it, if not oh well. Well….I won! I began my

MAX journey January 12, 2015. At the time of submitting this story I am in the home stretch of my 3rd challenge. I am down 20 lbs. and have gone from those size 15 pants to a size 8. I have tons of more energy and I truly look forward to going to class every day. I can keep up with my kids and sometimes find myself with more energy than them. Even more exciting than that, my sister and I have gotten closer than ever and we are opening our own MAX Challenge center! Not only have I gotten my life back, I have found the career I have always dreamed of! My fitness journey is far from over, and I sometimes still struggle with the nutrition and staying motivated. The difference now it that I know I have all of MAX nation to turn to for support. The MAX Challenge has changed my life forever and I am not looking back.

Amy Potpinka

MAX Transformation story #50

Amy Potpinka, MAX Transformation story #50 – Before and After picture

> ## "No pun intended, but the staff always 'had my back'."
> ### *- Diane Kellerhals*

My 'Success Story' is a little different than others. My story is more about the instructors at the East Windsor location than it is about me. In early December I injured my knee and in January, on 'Black Ice Sunday' I fell on my back on concrete steps. Anyone would have thought that with these injuries, physical activity would be out of the question. But not at MAX.

Although in pain, I was still mobile so I went to my classes. The MAX Culture of 'Personal Best' gave me the confidence to go to class each day and test myself while I recuperated. All I had to do was to let my instructors know the circumstances and my limitations and they did the rest. They checked with me often during classes to ensure I was OK. They always gave me modifications. They always encouraged me.

I do not believe there is another fitness facility, program or staff where I could experience these injuries and not miss a class. No pun intended, but the staff always 'had my back'. Their genuine concern was evident. They have created an environment that gave me the confidence to come to class and know I would not injure myself further and more importantly, that I could participate without judgement. On days when everyone was doings sit-ups and all I could do were leg raisers, I was encouraged by comments like 'Good Modification!' One instructor even stood in for me in some partner drills when she thought they might be too intense.

And the members were just as supportive. They gave me suggestions and when necessary, sympathy.

All of this is what makes MAX different. I can't thank the instructors and members at the East Windsor location enough.

Diane Kellerhals

MAX Transformation story #51

"MAX is not a diet nor a gym – it is a way of life and I am truly grateful that I got on board when I did."
- Rubin Mendelson

As I've always been overweight I've tried many diets and work-out routines – some with success, others not so much – but in the end it was always the "Yo Yo effect" put the weight back on plus some.

That has not been the case with The MAX Challenge.

I lost 90lbs in year 1 and now in year 3 I have kept almost all of it off while still attending the MAX of Manalapan 8:30pm class 5 nights a week.

I have also gotten off of my high blood pressure meds while creating a whole new "Me".

It is also a family affair as my wife attends class with me and my daughter is a member in Staten Island. My youngest son was also a MAX member and trainer until he moved away, with another son subsidizing my initial challenge knowing I needed to improve my health before disaster struck.

MAX is not a diet nor a gym – it is a way of life and I am truly grateful that I got on board when I did.

"Take It To The MAX"

Rubin Mendelson

MAX Transformation story #52

"I was dying and no one seemed to realize it."
- Scott Alboum

I was your typical guy in his thirty's. I was overweight and always ate junk food and fast food. Otherwise, I was generally healthy and never really thought too much about taking care of myself or working out. I never went to see a doctor either, even if I was sick. I usually would take some over the counter medication and be fine in a few days. That was pretty much how things went for me until the one time I got sick and didn't get better. I had a hole in my colon and didn't know it. I saw a number of doctors but they all misdiagnosed it. I ended up in the ER and eventually spent 21 days in the hospital and eventually needed emergency surgery. It took two years to recover from this ordeal. A year later, I thought I was better until I failed a physical exam and was diagnosed with type 2 diabetes. The type 2 diabetes diagnosis made me start thinking about my health in a different way. For a few months I dieted and monitored my blood sugar. But, after a while I fell back into my old ways and stopped taking care of myself. What I failed to realize then was that my immune system was damaged by my illness and that not taking care of myself meant I would be sick all of the time. While this was happening to me, my wife joined the MAX of Hamilton. She had been busy taking care of our kids and not herself. This was her chance to focus on her. It worked. She began to lose weight, get stronger and overall become very healthy. She became an inspiration to many people and some who watched her progress even signed up for the MAX. Except for me, I still didn't think I could do it. I watched from the sidelines as she excelled at the MAX of Hamilton and I was there with our kids when she was named the winner of a MAX Challenge this year. At that moment my entire life changed as I realized that she also inspired me. That's when I signed up for the MAX of Hamilton. Since then, I have worked out at the MAX over 70 times and I have only missed class when my family was on vacation. I have lost more than 15lbs and dropped two shirt and pants sizes. My type 2 diabetes is finally under control and I can keep my blood sugar at a normal level without medication. Being healthy, eating right and working out are now part of my lifestyle. The MAX has shown me that I can do anything that I want to. I enjoy working out every day and pushing myself physically to a point I never thought I could get to. The MAX has changed my life and I plan to continue living a healthy lifestyle.

Scott Alboum

MAX Transformation story #53

> *"So just because you are skinny doesn't mean you are healthy."*
> *- Theresa Clark*

Here I go Marc...everyone has a story and I can honestly say only one person in my life knows this story but you asked us to share, maybe it's part of the therapy. So as a 160 lb. kid I took mental abuse from kids and peers for what seemed like forever but probably was 10 years of my life. At the age of 20 I decided no more being made fun of...I joined WW and got to my goal of 120 pounds. Throughout the next 28 years, yes I'm 48, I went up and down 7-10 lbs. here and there but found myself starving to maintain my 120 lb. body. My body that I felt was fat. I created major health issues, destroyed my gallbladder and pancreas. Having to go 3 days without eating or drinking to avoid organ failure. For the past 5 years in and out of the hospital but I didn't care because I just wanted to be skinny. I joined the MAX to get myself in control, to learn how to eat. As you know I complained the first 3 weeks of all the food and I nearly gagged getting it all in but thanks to my partner Adrienne Burns Burmeister she kept telling me you have to do this. All I kept thinking was I'm going to gain weight but I kept on eating. After 5 weeks I can honestly say I'm eating all day and yes I still hate that but I'm doing it and I don't cheat I eat it all. I'm addicted to the workouts and I've lost 5 pounds. I have had no organ failure in 5 weeks and my body feels amazing. I still think I'm Fat but maybe the next 5 weeks will fix that unless Adrienne front hooks me in class tomorrow. So just because you skinny doesn't mean you are healthy. I'm hoping with The MAX I can live healthy for at least another 28 years!!!

Update: My 10 week challenge is complete....results: lost 10 lbs., lost a whole lots of inches, lost all health issues. Gained a lot of muscle and a livable healthy lifestyle! Thanks MAX!!!!

Theresa Clark

MAX Transformation story #54

"I was a 48-year old asthmatic with a bum knee and a bum shoulder, but I went."
- Rachelle St. Phard

I would like to share my MAX story with you. I am 48 years old. I have struggled with my weight all my adult life. I was an athlete in high school and still kept pretty active through college. After having a child at 20, I was over 200 pounds. There were a few times I dipped below that point. Once doing Weight Watchers, another due to stress. I've done Weight Watchers several times as well as Jenny Craig, Atkins, and too many to mention. I've done the gym thing over many years, cycled, yoga, Pilates and walking. All to no avail.

I really wanted to be active, but my large body as well as some orthopedic issues were holding me back. I've suffered from a bad low back since the early 90's. I also walked around for 30 years with a torn ACL that finally got bad enough in 2012 for me to have surgery on it. (Ironically, fixing the knee, fixed my back problem!) Recovery from that took over 6 months. Didn't have too much time to recover from that because I was, at the same time, having severe pain from a torn rotator cuff. I had surgery on that in 2013. Again, at least 6 months of recovery. Not a fun time. A few months into 2014, I ended up having my gall bladder removed (that too I was putting off and had known about for some time, but just couldn't take another surgery-then I had no choice). That was 3 surgeries in less than 2 years. I was a walking disaster area!

In January of 2015, I finally realized that if I didn't do something drastic, I was just going to keep getting fatter. I had topped the scale at 233 pounds, my all-time high. I had been seeing pictures of 3 people I knew whose lives were transformed by The MAX. Nestor Solis, who I knew from church, was dwindling before my eyes on Facebook. Kim Ziegler, whom I also knew from church, surprised me one day when I saw her. She was so fit and trim. She told me about The MAX and how she was an instructor and she loved it. She looked great. Also, my former walking partner, Lisa Grillo, who didn't lose any weight when we walked in the mornings, was also now trimming down. All of them inspired me to check out The MAX. I showed up one Saturday and signed up, as Kim cheered me on!

I started February 9th, 2015. Some of you many remember that around that time were some of the coldest days of the winter. Many mornings I recall looking at the temperature in my car and it reading 0 degrees as I made my way to the MAX. I was a 48-year old asthmatic with a bum knee and a bum shoulder, but I went. Several times that first week, I had to stop because it was too much or I just couldn't breathe. I pretty much did EVERYTHING modified, but THAT is the beauty of The MAX. I never felt like I was inferior or had to keep up with everyone (well, now I do, but not a first). My classmates made me feel comfortable and encouraged me to push what I could, but go at my own pace. I can honestly say that is one of the main reasons I love The MAX. You do it as you can and only what your body allows. I have done things I never thought I could, like jumping-jumping-jacks or running several laps, which I couldn't do in the beginning. Although I do still have knee issues that hold me back, I do what I can when I feel good and modify when I need to. Even modifying, you can lose and tone, EVEYRONE needs to know that so they are not discouraged when they are starting out.

The nutrition is such a key. I feel so much better now that I am eating cleaner. I do not have as many stomach issues and my frequent headaches are pretty much non-existent. For the most part, I really don't miss those old foods and when I do, I know I can have them for my treat meal.

I am so grateful to The MAX and how it has changed my life. I even got my husband to join and he is on this journey as well. I am now 203 pounds, 6 months later. I hope to lose 20-30 more over the coming year. Although I don't have measurements from before, I know I have lost substantial inches and gained muscle and strength! These 30 pound are just the beginning. I am NEVER going back! Thank you MAX Challenge!

Rachelle St. Phard

MAX Transformation story #55

> **"I was hostage to quick meals and carpools but deep down inside I knew that something had to change."**
> *- Melissa F*

This is how my story begins, I am just your average overworked wife and mother of 3.I made no time for myself and found every excuse as to why "me time" was impossible. I was hostage to quick meals and carpools but deep down inside I knew that something had to change. 5 1/2 months ago I made the decision to take control of my health. My goal was to get healthier, eat better and lose weight. Yes that's right losing weight was last on my list! I knew if I retrained my brain, structured my diet and got healthier that the weight loss would follow. In all actuality my goal was a change of lifestyle. Everyone has their defining moment and mine was not being able to function at the level I knew I was capable of and then finally stepping on a scale and shocked by the number I saw staring at me. Joining The MAX has helped me reach all the initial goals that I set forth for myself and for me there's no going back! I was asked when I first started what my weight loss goal was and I said 50 lbs., all the while thinking I would be happy losing 30lbs but knowing that I needed to lose more than the 50 lbs. I just reached my initial 50 lb. weight loss goal but my journey doesn't end here, I'm just getting started. I've applied all the tool that The MAX has taught me and now I'm ready to push myself to accomplish bigger goals and I'm excited to share my story in hopes that it motivates others. The MAX offers the best balance of motivation, nutrition guidance, and intense workouts. Find a MAX location near you and take a sample class...you won't regret it!

Forever thankful for this great program.

Melissa F

MAX Transformation story #56

I'VE COME TOO FAR AND WORKED TOO HARD TO EVER GO BACK!

Melissa F, MAX Transformation story #56 – Before and After picture

"I come for me and I come for them because we don't let each other down and we motivate and encourage each other."
- Cindy Bivians

I have Rheumatoid Arthritis and Fibromyalgia, which are autoimmune diseases. Almost 2 years ago I was at the peak of inflammation, chronic pain, depression and weight gain from not being able to move. I am taking low-dose chemotherapy medicine and protein blocking self-injections to try and stop my body from attacking itself.

I had an issue with balance, getting up from a seated position and was actually falling out of bed in the morning. It took almost 2 hours before my morning pain and stiffness subsided enough to be able to function and get to work. My doctor suggested a cane to assist in getting up and down and out of bed. The problem was my hands couldn't hold or grip the cane. I was at a loss.

Then my cousin-in-law told me about MAX and that an instructor has Rheumatoid and is able to get relief from moving. I agreed to a trial and was cautiously optimistic...at this point I had nothing to lose.

I could barely do any of the exercises. I felt like everyone is looking at me. I fell over. I saw myself in the mirror and was disgusted. People were high-fiving me and I thought they felt sorry for me. I absolutely could not hold a plank for more than 10 seconds. I made a terrible mistake coming here kept running through my head.

On the ride home I cried...then a strange thing happened -- I felt better. I felt better and that was enough to sign up.

I did everything modified and still do many things modified. I get up and down different than others...slower, awkward, whatever...I eventually get up. When I go to MAX I feel good and when I don't I feel awful. It's as simple as that. I love seeing my 6am crew each morning and I am consistently motivated, encouraged and challenged by my Trainer Katie. I come for me and I come for them because we don't let each other down and we motivate and encourage each other. I love hearing about their successes whether they are major or minor. First full-on burpee? Love to clap it up for you and tell you that you "smell delicious" (inside Old Bridge joke).

I started to go because it made my pain feel better and I thought that was my only goal. I didn't count on a body transformation and I never imagined how my entire outlook on life would change. I don't weigh myself regularly, however at my last physical I lost 22lbs and many inches. I've reduced my medicines and continue to find natural and nutritional ways to fight these diseases. Above all I smile more and I am happy. It was a transformation of me from the inside out.

I learned not to set imitations. There are no limits...only goals. I will be 50 years old in October and I've never felt better or been happier in my entire life. Love my MAX family.

Cindy Bivians

MAX Transformation story #57

'When my stomach passed my bra and stood out further than my chest I knew something had to happen."
- Karen Cofresi

In the last few years I had become very complacent with life and food. After a tough personal year (deaths, loss of job, surgery and family illness) I had turned to food as my comfort. My reasoning was well what if I die tomorrow, I didn't get to have dessert tonight. I reached my highest weight ever 230 pounds. I was having trouble walking even small amounts (running out of breath) and always restless (insomnia) at night. I felt awful and just kept buying bigger sizes, thinking I can hide behind these large clothes. When my stomach passed my bra and stood out further than my chest I knew something had to happen.

In January 2015 I moved to Florida and I started my own routine to lose weight. I lost nearly 30 pounds and then just plateaued. I had seen a friend of mine who lived in New Jersey had joined MAX Challenge and lost 26 pounds. She looked great! I searched for a MAX in Florida and there was none. In June after much thought I decided to move back to NY for several important reasons. One of which was to join MAX Challenge in Staten Island!

We arrived in NY mid-July and I must have called Jennifer at MAX Challenge a hundred times with all sorts of questions. My 49th birthday was July 26 and all I asked anyone for, was a membership to the MAX Challenge. I joined that Monday and am currently in my fourth week, even though most of the other members are in their 7th week. I love it! Since I joined I've lost an additional 15 pounds in 3 weeks! I feel healthier.

I look much better. I know I am getting stronger every single day. My stamina is out of control. I can walk and carry my twenty pound dog for long distances without getting winded. I eat, live and breathe MAX. My friends and family say I am obsessed and seem much happier and healthier. On weekends when there are no classes I am upset I can't attend a class, I feel like a part of my day is missing.

I feel myself getting stronger and stronger. I realized one day, on the floor sweating and rolling my eyes at the instructor, NO ONE, NO ONE but me was going to push me further except for myself. From that point on, I made a decision to bring everything I have to every single class and push myself just 15 more seconds, even when I think I can't go on any more.

The most surprising part of The MAX Challenge, was the overwhelming support from day one from not only the instructors, but the other classmates. They were in their fourth or fifth week, and stopped to make time, to help and encourage the newcomer. They are all so supportive of each other.

The instructors are all awesome and push you to do your best, but I have to say Chrissy Malone is just wonderful. Her energy and enthusiasm are contagious. She pushes you really hard in her class but makes you laugh and have fun throughout the torture! I love her classes! I had told some of the instructors there was no way I could do a sit up or push up. One day after class Chrissy asked me to stay behind a few minutes and helped me do a sit up and push up and gave advice on how to practice at home. I never thought I could do it and without her assistance I might have still thought that way. Now I can do pushups and a few sit-ups.

Lastly one of my most proud moments was this morning. I had never been able to plank. My first day I collapsed after 15 seconds. Tommy another instructor/classmate kept pushing me and telling me to go at my own pace, even if it took months. Well this morning I planked three minutes while my classmates and Tommy cheered me on!

MAX Challenge is not just an exercise plan, or diet. It's a family, a way of life. Everyone is so supportive and encouraging to each other. A month ago I couldn't do a sit-up, push-up nor plank and look how far I've come. I can't wait to see what I can accomplish in another month. I've never felt better, looked better or had the energy I have. Thank you to everyone at MAX I am now sleeping better and breathing easier. I am happy to say I am down from a size 24 to a 16 and I am running my first 5k in September with my new MAX family!

Karen Cofresi

MAX Transformation story #58

Karen Cofresi, MAX Transformation story #58 – Before and After picture

> '**I had no long term plan but I knew I had to make a change."**
> *- David Litty*

I am just an everyday guy who tried so many times the past decade to become the man he once was rather than a person he no longer recognized. Looking in the mirror at the end of 2013, I could not believe I had once been athletic or even a warrior, not only in the military sense but as in one who was self-disciplined in nutrition and fitness. However, after years of medications for anxiety (service related) that made me sedentary and tired all the time, as well as bad eating habits, I piled on the weight as heavy as 350 pounds at my heaviest in 2012. In November and December of 2013, I lost my vison for long periods and went blind three times, and I had no long term plan but I knew I had to make a change. I started January 1st 2014 at 297 pounds, wearing size 50 waist pants and size 3XL shirts. I began to eat less food at each meal and stopped gorging on second and third servings. I also started walking every day. I tried workout DVDs but could not get into working out alone; likewise, the local gym did not appeal to me as it was always crowded with fit people and I felt out of place as I stuck out as an obese person.

Finally, one day at the end of February, I checked my mail, and it contained a post card from a new program offered at Kovars Satori Academy of Martial Arts - Fair Oaks, CA called The MAX Challenge. It offered no short cuts or magical pills but promised results were typical and guaranteed. Looking at the picture of Christine, who had once been a real, obese person like myself, I decided I had nothing to lose. The people I met at the kick off, Michelle Zeillemaker, Elaine Warrener, Bryan Klein, Marisol Cardella, and many others convinced me to give it a shot. I started my first my first challenge weighing 277 pounds, wearing size 48 waist pants and 3XL shirts, and it was the hardest work I had done physically since basic training as a young man, and at times I had to modify as I could not do a sit up, Jumping Jack, or more than a few pushups; however, I made plenty of new friends who motivated and encouraged me to do my best. I stayed with it, and ten weeks later, I had progressed to where I had more agility and could move more. Moreover, I was honored when my trainers and friends selected me as a co-finalist and winner of $500 for The MAX Challenge at Kovars, Fair Oaks, CA. at the end of that first challenge. I have watched my confidence grow as the first week of my second challenge I found myself able to do real pushups and sit ups where I used momentum of my arms to throw myself forward, and during my third challenge I finally became able to do real sit ups without having to throw my arms forward for momentum.   I am almost done with my seventh challenge now, and I do not even recognize myself a year and four months since starting The MAX Challenge: I lost 110 pounds total in 2014, 90 pounds of it while on the MAX Challenge, where I went from 277 to 187 pounds, and my waist went from size 48 with top button undone down to a size 36 and 34 while my shirt went from 3XL down to L/XL as I prefer loose shirts. My doctor gave me a clean bill of health after last month's physical and was impressed with the changes in my cholesterol and sugar levels as well as blood pressure levels. Words simply cannot express the inner changes I have went through as well as the physical changes thanks to The MAX Challenge: I am no longer on medication for anxiety or depression; I find myself more confident in my daily activities, and the people I know socially or at work notice a positive change in my overall attitude, not to mention all the comments I get from coworkers and friends about how I am a total-ly different person than the one I used to be. Thank You MAX Challenge.

David Litty

MAX Transformation story #59

> *"I call it The Creep. Every year, a few extra pounds creep onto your body."*
> *- Andrew Feldman*

Hello, I've been a member of the Springfield NJ chapter since its opening. Here's a post I wrote at the end of my first challenge. Feel free to use any or none of it--I know there are a lot of great stories out there.

You don't notice it at first, then you can't help but not notice it. Because not only are your clothes tighter, but your cholesterol is a little higher, you have less patience, and you can't always keep up with your kids.

I knew I needed a change, but most programs seemed too intense or too limiting. Then a friend and fellow suburban dad/desk jobber got great results with The MAX, so I decided to try it.

I think the MAX works because it combines the best parts of many other fitness programs: the accountability of a personal trainer, the community of CrossFit, the intensity of a P90X video, and the positive energy of Zumba. And because they offer multiple classes per day, my wife and I could both join, follow the nutrition, and motivate one another.

Bottom line: after 9 weeks, I'm down 26 lbs. and 12 inches. I sleep better, I'm more productive at work, and I'm a lot happier with how I look. That's why--even though we're on vacation next week--we'll still

FaceTime into class every day.

Thank you to the owners, trainers, and all my fellow MAX ers for pushing me. Because when you see a difference and conquer The Creep, it feels pretty great.

Andrew Feldman

MAX Transformation story #60

Andrew Feldman, MAX Transformation story #60 – Before and After picture

> **"When I felt myself start to go down the wrong path I looked at picture of what I looked like and remembered why I started."**
> *- Andrea Vindigni*

just completed my second challenge with the MAX and could not be happier. I started the MAX on March 30th right after my 24th birthday. I tried every diet under the sun, you name it I did it. From Weight Watchers to Slim Fast, which put me in the hospital with stomach problem, to Jenny Craig and South Beach Diets. I googled diets, cut out certain foods and even tried to exercise every day. In college I was on the Tyra Banks show for teens who were self-conscious about their weight and that was the first time I was public about being self -conscious. I am a really outgoing, life loving person, but I also kept my insecurities to myself. When I heard about the MAX I was skeptical, I thought it would be like every other diet that I tried. I quickly learned that the MAX isn't a diet, it is a life style change. When I took my first before picture I was disgusted, how I could ever let myself get to the size I was really opened my eyes. At 24 years old and 5'2 I weighed 274 pounds and wore sizes ranging from a XXL to a size 20 or 22 in pants. Needless to say I fit the "morbidly obese" category at every doctor I saw.

I started the MAX in full force. I busted my butt and completed my first challenge with perfect attendance. The beginning was a slow change and it took every ounce of my 274 pound body to stay compliant. When I felt myself start to go down the wrong path I looked at picture of what I looked like and remembered why I started. The instructors were extremely inspirational and the fact that my mom and I started this journey together made me push even more. Slowly but surely I started to see results, and so did everyone around me. I let this act as my motivation. In class, I encouraged everyone and made sure that they didn't give up, that we were almost at the end. I clapped it up for everyone and made sure I shouted out everyone's name in class at least once, so in case they had any doubts that they couldn't do it, I assured them that they could. After all as the instructors say, "You can do anything for 10 seconds."

I ended my first challenge as the semi-finalist for my class for the big $1,000 prize. Unfortunately I was not deemed the winner of the MAX Challenge but it became so much more for me that just being a "winner." I was a winner to myself, I completed 10 weeks, 50 workouts, and a HUGE change in my diet. After finishing my first challenge I went down 2 sizes and 27 pounds. I completed every day of the legacy weeks and started my second challenge just as strong as the first one. I just completed my second challenge and that last week of legacy another 2 sizes down and 32 more pounds down. With a total loss of 59 pounds in 23 weeks I am overjoyed. I worked so hard to be where I am. The beginning was tough, the scale stayed the same and I was discouraged. I learned to stay off the scale and just do my own thing, when I wasn't losing weight I was gaining muscle. I am so much stronger and healthier than I have ever been! I brought many people to the MAX to help them get on the right path and I love seeing everyone's transformation. I am not where I want to be yet and still have a long way to go, but without the MAX I wouldn't be where I am today. It's not easy, it takes heart, dedication, and willingness to change, but it is worth it. Let my success story inspire others, especially girls my own age who may be in the same position as me. The MAX no only changed my life but saved it.

Andrea Vindigni

MAX Transformation story #61

> **"I was so intrigued by the program because of the comradery that surrounded it."**
> *- Tahitia Jones-Whitfield*

I've struggled with my weight my entire life. Every diet you can think of, I've tried it. The yo-yo dieter that was me. I'd lose 30 pounds and gain 45 pounds back. Finally after being sick and tired of being sick and tired, I started my lifetime fitness journey. I spoke with my doctor, hooked up with a nutritionist and joined the gym. I would work out about two hours a day, five days a week. I did get results, but I was killing myself to get them. After about six months, I hit a plateau. I would be in the gym every day, go walking at the track in the morning and the evening, and the scale wouldn't budge. That lasted about six weeks and I realized I had to do something different.

I had heard about The MAX through different Facebook posts. I watched some of the videos on their website and read some of the testimonies. I was so intrigued by the program because of the comradery that surrounded it. I never thought I was one of those people that needed that pat on the back, but I guess I was wrong. At the gym, there's no one cheering you on, pushing you to go to the next level. I knew it was the program for me. Nutrition counseling and killer workouts in one location for 45 minutes, I was sold!!! So while on vacation, I called and signed up over the phone for a challenge that had already begun.

I've been hooked ever since. In the very beginning, I wasn't sure if I could do it. But I just kept telling myself, it's only 10 weeks, it's only 10 weeks. And before I knew it, the challenge was over. I was down 18 pounds and 17 ½ inches. Currently, I'm in week 8 of my second challenge and I'm already down 20 pounds.

I've never been so committed to anything in my life. The owners, trainers, classmates and FB group are really like an extended family. Every day I have been either encouraged or inspired by someone in the program. I'm stronger today than I've ever been and although there's still progress to be made, I know that I will reach my fitness goals. This group pushes each and every one of us to do better than the day before…to be our best selves. I can say without a shadow of a doubt, I'm a better person today because of The MAX.

Tahitia Jones-Whitfield

MAX Transformation story #62

"The benefits go far beyond weight loss."
- Barbara St. John

As in all good stories, I will start at the beginning. I was on a fad "cookie" diet and had lost 40 pounds eating a cookie every 3 hours and exercising. When I went back to eating food, I promptly put 20 pounds back on.

The MAX of Manalapan was new and they were having a "sprint" challenge from the end of November till end of Dec.

I met with Brian Klein who explained the program and encouraged me to try it. He did not push it and I joined as a non-believer. Well, as they say, the rest is history.

I started at 210 pounds and a size 18-20.

I am 3 years in this November and not only have I lost 50 pounds, but I continue to keep it off. That is the difference with this program. The nutrition has become a way of life just as exercising 6 days a week has.

I am a solid size 10 (my dream was a size 12) and I just wore a size 6 dress to a wedding last weekend.

I tell people if you don't see me at class, I'm either bike riding, swimming, or running. I weigh myself every morning to stay on track and allow myself a treat meal every weekend. What I have accomplished has not come easily but it has been worth every penny, jumping jack, and drop of sweat.

The benefits go far beyond weight loss. I have a level of energy that I have not had in many years and am more confident than ever. I have run a marathon and just completed an Olympic triathlon. Last September I changed jobs, leaving a negative environment and have returned to school for my bachelors.

After getting up every morning for 5am class for almost a year, my husband joined. He too has lost 50 pounds and is down to his wedding day weight. We eat cleanly and exercise together. I think it's the energy level that impresses me the most. We are definitely making great strides to a healthy lifestyle.

Since January my daughter has joined MAX. She has lost almost ten pounds but more importantly, she exercises regularly and eats healthier than in the past.

I have heard many people speak against the program. Many say it's too expensive or it's unreasonable to exercise every day. I feel that if you go to class and follow the nutrition it is well worth the fee. The American Heart Association recommends daily exercise. I challenge anyone to take it to the MAX for 10 weeks. You will be very pleased with both the internal and external results.

I don't see me walking away from the program anytime soon and continue to enjoy being fabulous!

Barbara St. John

MAX Transformation story #63

"I so desperately wanted to lose the weight, but I didn't know how to do it"
- Lauren Weissberg

I 've struggled with my weight for as long as I can remember. Back in high school, my mother always told me that I would be so pretty if I "just lost 20 pounds"...so, I tried...and failed. And gained more weight. Then I tried...and failed again...and gained more weight. Before I knew it, those 20 pounds became 30, then 40, then 50, and finally, about 75. I have tried every diet out there. Nutrisystem, Jenny Craig, Weight Watchers, South Beach, Atkins. Seriously--you name it, I've tried it. You can buy a pill that will help you lose weight? Great, I'll take two bottles! I so desperately wanted to lose the weight, but I didn't know how to do it. I would swear I was going to start on Monday, but then Monday came and went I had a gym membership, but I was the best kind of client--paid my money every month and never showed up. I wanted a quick fix. A magic pill. A shake to drink that would make all of my excess weight go away as quickly as possible. If I couldn't get instant gratification, why bother? It would take too long to lose the weight, I reasoned...and then became filled with regret when time passed and I realized I had done nothing to help my cause. I knew that time was creeping up on me and I didn't know how much longer I could get away with being the healthiest fat person I knew. I have a loving husband and two beautiful sons that I want to be here for. I wanted to walk up the stairs without being winded, or play outside with them for hours on end. I didn't just want to be alive--I wanted to live. And for the first time in 35 years, I was ready.

I learned about The MAX from local moms and was incredibly impressed when I went for my consultation. I really lacked a good nutritional foundation (I mean, my mom served powdered doughnuts as breakfast when I was a kid) and this was so reasonable to follow. I immediately went food shopping and began to prepare for this new journey. I decided on the 5AM class because I hate exercise more than I like eating, and I figured if I did the class the first thing in the morning, I would have no excuse later on. I don't think my husband thought I would be able to get up at 4AM, exercise, get ready for work, work a whole day, then come home and take care of the family and the house. Frankly, I wasn't so sure either. But I had to try. My first class...I was so nervous. I joined on week 4 of a challenge, so I got to do a burpee on my very first day. Was I graceful? I was not. But I did it. I really thought I would not survive that first class, but I did. Everyone there was so welcoming and encouraging on that first day, but it did not stop there. The support I get from my center owners Allison & Amy, my trainer Mak, and my classmates never ends. They make me want to work harder, and I do! But perhaps the best thing to come out of this 5AM class was my permanent partner, Judy. She adopted me in my second week and we have been inseparable ever since. We are truly fitness equals (oh, the irony!) and push one another in the most positive of ways. She truly inspires me and makes me want to work harder.

Since joining The MAX, I have learned to make better food choices, eat proper portions, cook delicious and healthy meals, learn to love exercise, and not to be afraid to try something new. I am devoted to my new lifestyle and would rather bring a bag full of my own compliant meals to a party and field questions from everyone around me than risk falling off the wagon. I was also able to complete my first 5K--something I had been talking about doing for a long time, but didn't believe I could actually accomplish. I am proud to report that my first 10 week challenge resulted in the loss of 22 pounds and 22 inches. I am currently in week 8 of my second challenge and I can't wait to see what comes next. Mak always tells us to remember our "why" as we move through this journey. My "why" is my family--my husband and my two sons, and I will keep fighting for my why for as long as it takes.

The rest is still unwritten...

Lauren Weissberg

MAX Transformation story #64

> "I finally found the right mix of nutrition and exercise to help me lose weight and optimize my health."
> *- Sheli Monacchio*

My story begins way before I am choosing to begin mine here. I have been struggling with weight since 2001 when I broke my ankle and tore my ACL all in the same year. I have struggled with my self-image for much longer than that. Comfort comes from food in our Italian family and emotionally speaking, with some of the things I have faced in my life, what I ate was the only thing I was able to control.

When I got engaged to Keith I had a 19 and a 21 year old. We discussed having children (he hadn't had any at this point) and I wanted to give him that gift but didn't really think I would be able to. After 18 months, we needed some hormone support to be able to conceive and we took the IVF route. Before we even got pregnant, I gained 15 lbs. just from the hormones.

Out of that experience we have been blessed with an 11lb. 12 oz. baby boy born on May 30th of 2013. (Yes I had gestational diabetes) I was a type II diabetic for the past ten years.

Keith and I had similar epiphanies at the same time on how important it was to get our health in check. I had terrible eczema and a toe surgery that wouldn't heal for months. And I was exhausted all the time. With a two year old, that could cause a problem.

We made a commitment to ourselves and each other that we would get healthy in order to be the best "us" for our little boy and so we can have a long life together.

Keith called the MAX Challenge to get some information since he kept seeing and hearing about it. He signed up right then. I wasn't sure I would be able to due to my job, the baby, my other kids and all of the other responsibilities that I have.

When I spoke to Jennifer on the phone, she deflected every excuse I had and I ended up signing up with her. My first day, she joined me to exercise in my first class to show support. I was terrified thinking I would fail at this like so many other times. But the truth is for me, those other plans failed me.

I finally found the right mix of nutrition and exercise to help me lose weight and optimize my health. After two weeks, my eczema completely disappeared and my toe healed.

It has only been 7 weeks now, but I haven't had this much energy in YEARS. I haven't felt "healthy" in 20 years. My sugar is under control and I no longer need medication.

I am down 21 lbs. as of today with three weeks to go in my first challenge. I no longer say I don't have time for me. I have to make time for me in order to care for everyone else. For the first time in my life, I am a priority to myself.

Thank you for this gift and a wonderful life lesson MAX Challenge. I look forward to leaving my legacy.

Sheli Monacchio

MAX Transformation story #65

> ## "I am a changed person (both in body and mind) and hope to MAX as long as I can move! "
> ### - Kathryn M. Noonan

I am a diabetic who had a heart attack in March 2015, and had two stents inserted. After I was cleared to come back to work, I began my MAX journey. The good news is that in the first 10 weeks, I lost 16 ½ inches and went from a size 12 to a size 8! Now for the great news (yes it gets better). I just received my latest blood-work results. My AC-1 is down from a 9.3 to a 6.5. It has never been lower. My cholesterol and triglyceride levels are all NORMAL, and they have not been normal for 3 years!!! My Dr. is taking me off one of my blood pressure medications AND one of my diabetes meds!!!!I owe this all to the MAX Challenge. Thanks Joe for initiating the program in the County and thank you to Allison and Amy and all the awesome trainers for motivating me so much. I am a changed person (both in body and mind) and hope to MAX as long as I can move!

Kathryn M. Noonan

MAX Transformation story #66

> "The physical challenges I have embraced since embarking on my MAX journey have afforded me opportunities I never knew could be on my radar."
> *- Ashley Chuchla*

After the fifth time asking my husband, "Did you dry these?" I knew I had been in denial long enough. My MAX journey began in June 2014 and, more than one year later, my entire outlook on fitness, nutrition, and my own personal happiness has been infinitely transformed. Shedding 20lbs, dropping two pant sizes, and building inches of muscle has allowed me to exude confidence I haven't felt since my time as a college swimmer.

Most notably, the physical challenges I have embraced since embarking on my MAX journey have afforded me opportunities I never knew could be on my radar. Three months after joining the MAX of Springfield, I jogged my first official 5K. A month later, I ran my first 10K, and by the following February I ran a 10K + half marathon challenge. These feats would not have been achievable without the MAX fitness and nutrition program, and for that my commitment is unwavering and my appreciation eternal.

Ashley Chuchla

MAX Transformation story #67

> '**I give you two thumbs up for helping me to improve my health and overall well-being. "**
> *- Aldo Mancilla*

HOW "THE MAX" TRANSFORMED MY LIFE

My name is Aldo Mancilla and I'm 51 years old. My wife (Wendy) was starting her first challenge and wanted me to join as well. I was very skeptical and really not interested. She asked if I would at least support her by attending the kick off which I agreed to. Lee Grebler talked to me after the kickoff and guaranteed me that I could indeed get through the exercises and that there were modifications for all levels. They arranged for me to take a sample class the first day of the challenge and the rest is history. The MAX has truly been life changing.

In 2008 I suffered a stroke and in 2010 I underwent a double lung transplant. Since I've joined the MAX it has given me more stamina, endurance and even my balance has improved (equilibrium damage from my stroke). I also suffer from back and leg pain.

I attend class every day at 5 am and then head to my job with an hour plus commute. I'm on my second challenge (joined 3/30/15) and have lost 35 pounds and many inches. I owe a large part of my success to two tremendous ladies, my wife and most of all Elissa Grebler (instructor and owner of Howell). My wife prepares all of my food and keeps me on point with the nutrition. Elissa pushes you through the exercises by making it fun and most of all encouraging you. She also has something that my wife and I always talk about, her compassion for what she does and her genuine interest in each and every member. Elissa is a true leader and that is something that can't be taught. I give you two thumbs up for helping me to improve my health and overall well-being.

Thank you MAX of Howell!!

Aldo Mancilla

MAX Transformation story #68

> **"This was my wake-up call."**
> *- Amanda Lupinacci*

My name is Amanda Lupinacci and I am 25 years old. I started my first challenge, Week 1 Day 1 on September 29, 2014. I walked in the doors of the MAX of Hamilton for the 7pm class knowing only one person in the entire class. I was nervous, but thought to myself, "You are the youngest in here, you use to play soccer for the majority of your life, and you got this"! Boy was I wrong! I ended up having to sit out more than half of the workout because I was on the verge of passing out. I was physically exhausted. This was my wake-up call. I needed to get back into being active and needed to change my ways in order to live a healthier life. Fast forwarding to today, I am in my fourth challenge coming up on the end of Week #8 and I have seen so many changes in my life, physically and mentally. I am down in weight, down in sizes, able to complete a full workout, have corrected some health issues that had been going on prior to the MAX, and have gained a positive attitude toward myself and toward working out. In this time, I have had an overall boost in my confidence. In addition to these changes, I have also become a happier, healthier, determined individual that is on a mission to stay healthy and never go back down the old road of bad habits. It is just shy of my year anniversary with the MAX, and I could not be more excited to say that this has been the longest amount of time I have ever committed to a fitness program. I would say I have been so successful in my MAX journey because I have taken it on as a lifestyle change, just the way the MAX is intended to be, and have an strong support system starting with my amazing instructors and continuing with my fellow MAXers. If there is one thing I would change about joining the MAX it would be to have joined sooner!

Amanda Lupinacci

MAX Transformation story #69

"Lots of clapping and high fives reminded me of the fun days when I had played basketball and I love the team spirit."
- Mary Valinotti

This past September was the first school year in fourteen years that all five of my children, Danielle, my twins, Michael and Christopher, Nicholas, and Justin, were all in school for the full day. Last year, my youngest, Justin, started kindergarten and if I had a dollar for every time someone asked me, "What are you doing with yourself with all that free time now?" I would be a millionaire! My schedule was packed with practices, activities, and events for my children's sports and three different schools. At the conclusion of a fun-filled summer last year, I made the decision to drive over to The MAX of Old Bridge. I walked in and asked some questions. Luckily, my soon-to-be mentor Priscilla McRae was at the entrance to greet me and told me to register for the September 2014 Challenge. I wondered how I was going to get there every weekday and hoped 10:00 a.m. would be the ideal class time for me. I made the commitment to look at my MAX class as if it was my job that I needed to show up to every day and excel in. When I started the nutrition plan that my instructors proposed to me, I felt and wound up looking so different. I never had stepped into Whole Foods, a supermarket of healthy foods and goods, before or shopped in the gluten-free section. This was such a change because I had gotten myself in the habit of grabbing quick meals at fast-food drive thru's with my children. As soon as I walked in the doors at MAX, the staff and even legacy members walked right over to me and started friendly conversations. I immediately friended the MAX Facebook page and right away legacy members were reaching out sending requests, recipes, and motivational quotes. Lots of clapping and high fives reminded me of the fun days when I had played basketball and I love the team spirit. The changes in the workouts kept me interested and challenged. I promised myself that I was going to make time for me. I told myself: A 45-minute class is not a lot! It's not even an hour! Its 10 weeks. The time line of week 1 -10 motivated me that each day I was closer to the end of week 2, week 3, closer to week 10. The goals I set for myself were to get there every day. To follow the nutritional guidelines. Shop for myself and prepare my foods. To get those 7 vegetables in. Each morning I made a protein shake. This was the first time that I ever bought protein powder and I was so happy that I could just purchase it right at The MAX. I started adding one cup of spinach, now I even have four cups. My husband, Michael is helping make in the morning and having them also. I began to turn down plans people were making for me for things I didn't enjoy doing! I began prioritizing and valuing my time. I was definitely not going to miss my MAX appointment at 10. After I did my workout, I didn't mind as much driving to all of the activities and events. I felt accomplished and happy that I did something for myself. My instructor had me set fitness goals in class: to kick over the boxing bag, 10 solid push-ups, Plank balancing on one medicine ball then 2 then 3! I want my children to be proud of me and to know I'm working hard. They influence me, with their work ethic and athleticism. I think of my sons doing their jumping jacks and burpees at their karate dojo. I'm motivated when I think of my daughter dancing 12 hours a week and kicking her leg up so high. I also want to be the girl I was when I was younger I Loved going to the gym and was in shape and even Coached basketball. MAX is helping me to believe in myself and take on more roles. I just volunteered as my son's basketball coach this past season and had the best time. I'm surrounding myself with positivity and with Inspiring people. This spring a group of us MAX moms joined together and registered for our first mud race. We are into our third one already! The camaraderie that we shared was so amazing, that I became a coach for our MAX class. I'm now looking forward to passing my instructor certification and teaching classes. I'm so grateful to MAX for helping me make my health and fitness a priority. I am able now to fit myself into my busy day's schedule. I was inspired, I believed, I achieved, now I inspire, believe in others, and achieve all of my goals. I have a fresh start; a new challenge is starting in a couple of weeks. I have my list of new goals and I'm excited to see where it takes me.

I didn't mention that I won the September 2014 Challenge at Old Bridge. But I'm proud of that!

Mary Valinotti

Mary Valinotti, MAX Transformation story #70 – Before and After picture

> "What a precious gift the MAX has turned out to be for me...it's the gift that keeps on giving!"
> *- Terri Hindes*

Why the MAX saved my life...

In 2007, life was wonderful! I was at the gym 4-5 times a week, I turned 40, was in the best shape of my life, had a wonderful job...and met Teddy, who eventually became my husband. In 2008, I was diagnosed with Breast Cancer, and underwent a radical mastectomy and chemotherapy to combat the Cancer. Not going to lie...losing my hair was hard, but it wasn't the hardest part – no, it was the fatigue and the weight gain from the medicine I needed to be on for the next 5 years that took its toll on my body and my mind.

I started a new job in 2010, and there were 4 men in my office all doing the MAX Program. They all lost a considerable amount of weight and I was envious, knowing that they were in a gym working out and doing what I loved to do – EXERCISE. Once I finished my medicine in 2014, they decided to get together and give me the greatest gift...a 10-week MAX program. From Challenge 1, day 1, I knew this place was different than what I had come to learn of exercise, coupled with the nutrition and friendly environment of recognition and appreciation.

I am proud to say that after only 1 year, I am down 3 dress sizes, have lost approximately 35 lbs. and am feeling wonderful again! Being healthy is a state of mind, not only from the outside, but from within. My husband and my step-son have both tried the program, and they are both on their way to living healthier lifestyles too, thanks to the MAX program! My goal weight is close – and I look forward to putting on that outfit that I wore on my 40th birthday (yes I still have it) to prove that everything is possible with hard work and determination – Setbacks happen, so you just have to make a new plan and reset! That's what I'm doing – and I will succeed! What a precious gift the MAX has turned out to be for me...it's the gift that keeps on giving!

Terri Hindes

MAX Transformation story #71

"I joined as a way of working though the daily stresses of my business."
- David Fine

I began March 30th at 198 pounds, I did not look overweight at 6'1", but felt uncomfortable in my own skin. I work with factories in China. I am usually awake and on skype at 4am reviewing production schedules and samples. By 5:30am my stress is MAX ed-and off to the MAX I go.

By the end of the challenge I reached my weight goal, to be under 180, I weighed in at 176. I was satisfied.

On August 19th I had my annual physical. My doctor was very surprised when reviewing my blood work and noting I dropped 23 pounds (now 175)

Total Cholesterol dropped 40 points from 230 (unhealthy) to 190 (very good)

LDL (Bad Cholesterol) dropped 30 points from 147(Bad) to 117 (normal)

Sugar level was pre-diabetic at a fasting level of 135, now at 75, low/normal

BMI dropped from 26.3 to 19 low/normal.

Blood Pressure at the last physical 140/90 Hypertension Stage 1, now it is 115/75-good/normal.

EKG, excellent, as were all of the other exams. My physician was very pleased.

I attribute these changes to the MAX Challenge and Noel. Her perky smile, quirky humor, constant enthusiasm and daily "Morning' Mr. Fine" keep me coming back. Thank you Noel.

David Fine, 56

MAX Transformation story #72

> "I needed to keep moving, to keep pushing, and the only way I was going to do that was if I had people around me watching me."
> *- Denise Meyer*

As I sat in my car on a warm September morning last fall, I was eating a pork roll, egg and cheese on a bagel and washing it down with a Nestle Quik chocolate milk. I only had about 5 minutes before I had to head in to my first MAX kick off meeting. I couldn't get that bagel in my mouth fast enough. As I sat there alone in my car, I wondered, what the heck am I doing here? I started to regret signing up over a month ago. Why did I do this? How am I ever going to do this? I weighed over 300 pounds and I could barely climb the two flights of stairs to my condo without peeing my pants from being so winded. But I knew I had to change my life otherwise, I was going to eat myself to death, as it was, and I was 38 and had been on high blood pressure for several years.

I didn't expect the kick-off meeting to cause so much stress and anxiety, I really thought that would be saved for the first day of class. As I sat through the kick-off and listened to everyone's positive and upbeat messages, I just felt more cynical. In fact, I was really beginning to regret my decision to join the MAX. I made a decision to commit to the challenge for the 10 weeks but after that, I would stop going. By the luck of the draw, I wound up with Tank as my instructor. I can honestly say that I'm not sure I would have done as well without her. By the end of the first week, I asked her to keep me as her student for the year. I have never committed to a lifestyle change for more than a couple of weeks, so to commit for one year was a rather lofty goal after only a few days and yet here I am, almost a full year later, a MAX devotee.

When I went into class on the first day, I put myself in the front row in the center of the room. I didn't really want to be there, I had to be there. I needed to keep moving, to keep pushing, and the only way I was going to do that was if I had people around me watching me. If I hid in the corner or the back of the room, I know that I would slack off and just not challenge myself as much as I should or could. I had no idea how difficult it would be but I told myself to just keep going. Luckily, I wrote much of my journey down in the beginning and I know that my progress was almost immediately evident. By the end of the week, I was stepping out less jumping jacks and managing to actually do the low kicks instead of stepping them out too. Right now, it is hard to believe I could not do a full sit-up when I began and I had to do push-ups on the wall, but it is true. I didn't start doing push-ups on my knees until the end of my first challenge, now I can handle 10 or 12 full pushups before I switch to my knees and sit-ups, well, I have no idea when I started full sit-ups, but I can't remember not being able to do them! My progress through my first challenge was remarkable but the moment that strikes me as the most empowering is the board break-ing. I was so nervous that I couldn't break my board that when I finally did go and the board broke, well, I will never forget that feeling, the belief that for the first time in my life, I am going to break through the diet mentality and begin living a healthy and active lifestyle was finally rooted deep inside of me.

At the end of my first challenge, I was incredibly honored by my class-mates to be selected as the finalist for our class. I was even more humbled and grateful to the MAX of Hazlet staff when they selected me as their inaugural challenge winner. Throughout my journey, I have had countless people tell me how inspiring I am to them. I find it so incredibly humbling. We all walked in the door for the same reason, to better ourselves. My in-spiration to join last August was the desire to have enough energy to pass the bar exam when I took it in February. I feel proud to say that I passed both the NY and NJ bar exams with the help of the MAX.

I am grateful for all of my success over the past year. Success is hard to measure, it is not always quantitative. I have lost over 60 pounds, a lot of inches, and my BMI has dropped 10 points. I know longer take blood pressure medicine. But my success is found in my positive attitude, my desire to keep maintaining a healthy and active lifestyle, and the progress I see in my level of fitness. Buying smaller clothing and receiving compliments on my success is also incredibly encouraging. My journey is ongoing and I will continue taking it to the MAX until I reach my goal.

Denise Meyer

MAX Transformation story #73

> ## "I have learned to use exercise to de-stress."
> ### *- Conswaila Diggs*

My name is Conswaila Diggs; I joined the MAX of Hamilton September 29, 2014. I just like many others have tried everything to lose weight some things with success and some without; I have been on my weight loss journey mentally since 2008. I say mentally because my mind was made up and I had decided that I would no longer try to take short cuts to obtain the results that I desired. I knew that I did not have all the pieces to the puzzle however; when I was told about the MAX Challenge in June of 2014 it all came together. I needed to work on Mind, Body & Spirit.

During my first challenge my weight loss was at a plateau and I was excited to see how the MAX would work for me. By the end of my first challenge I was down 12 pounds and a lot of inches. I felt better, slept better and had more energy. I knew by the third week of my first challenge that I would continue on the program for life. During my journey at the MAX I have lost weight and inches but most importantly my blood pressure has begun to normalize and I have learned to use exercise to de-stress. I have learned what to eat and what not to eat. I have learned when to eat and when not to eat. Nutrition is 80% of the puzzle this was my biggest issue! It did not matter how much I worked out if I did not give my body the proper nutrition it would not transform.

I have learned that no matter what is going on to set aside time for me; my time is my 45 minutes at the MAX. From day to day from inspirational quote to words of encouragement I have found new ways to take a look on the inside and how to address the negativity around me so that I can make the necessary changes on the outside. As I continue on this journey here at The MAX, I will continue to work on my Mind, Body & Spirit and help others do the same.

Thank you MAX for thinking outside of the box and bringing the total package which yields RESULTS!!!

Conswaila Diggs

MAX Transformation story #74

"The MAX truly is a great program and I am thankful that it appeared in my Facebook feed at just the right time. I was ready!!!"
- Melissa Greenberg

After many years of joining gyms and trying diets, I always found myself at the beginning again. Sure, I'd go for a while and even enjoyed some of the classes, but I never connected with anyone. None of the instructors knew me by name. I was just one of a number of people through the revolving door. Without anyone holding me accountable, I would go less and less until I was only "donating" to the facility and not actually using it.

After have 2 kids and knowing that was it for me, I wanted to make a new start. The MAX kept appearing in my Facebook feed and after a bunch of times, I decided to call and ask about it. I was impressed by what I heard on the phone but what really got me was the invitation to go try a sample class at the West Windsor location. Hamilton, where I live, wasn't opened yet.

I enjoyed the class and got a chance to ask the people there about their own experiences. Everyone was very positive and I loved the work out. I called back the next day and signed up for the Hamilton location. I was in the inaugural group of people at Hamilton. We all showed up on the first day not knowing exactly what to expect and not knowing each other or the instructors at all.

I stuck with it and am SO proud of myself. For 9 months, that's 3 strait challenges, I went 5 days a week (with a few exceptions) and actually made a difference. I made friends, I got to know the instructors very well and they got to know me. I lost 2 pants sizes and had more energy and felt stronger than ever. I felt so strong that I signed up and completed my first 5K race and ran it in about 35 minutes.

The MAX truly is a great program and I am thankful that it appeared in my Facebook feed at just the right time. I was ready!!!

Melissa Greenberg

MAX Transformation story #75

> *"It is a place I can go with no judgement and a ton of support and real direction with real food and real goals."*
> *- Donna Paprota*

Hi, my name is Donna Paprota, and I joined The MAX just 14 weeks ago. I am an average woman who is average height and never really had a weight problem until after my third child. When in my thirties, I started searching for a weight-loss plan. I tried all the popular programs like Jenny Craig, Nutri-System, Atkins, and South Beach to name a few. Of course, I lost some weight but only to gain it back and more. The yo-yo dieting and weight gain was really taking a toll on my body. I started having problems with my knees; mostly with my left knee as it would crack and pop whenever I went up a set of stairs or bent over. I know my weight had a lot to do with the pain in my knees. I then reached out to my family doctor, and I asked if there was anything that could aid me in my weight loss quest. Unfortunately, he said "Yes." I say unfortunately, because the pills he prescribed turned out to be dangerous. The doctor prescribed a weight loss medication that is now known to cause heart problems. The medication worked initially. It was easy, since I simply didn't eat, as the medicine took away my hungry. Well, eventually I built a tolerance for the medicine, and it stopped working; I was left feeling hopeless.

I am now in my mid-forties. I gradually gained more weight to reach nearly 200 pounds. My weigh-in weight at The MAX was 194 pounds nearly 14 weeks ago. I've come to realize all my other attempts at losing weight all had one thing in common, they were all a short-term gimmick with prepackaged food and no real direction. Just a few short days of going to The MAX, I started feeling like I had discovered something amazing. It is a place I can go with no judgement and a ton of support and real direction with real food and real goals.

I have experienced some physical setbacks along the way, but I am determined to get back to the body I once had. About three weeks into my journey, my bad knees where really hurting. It was so bad that I actually starting crying in class. I wasn't sure if I was crying from the pain or crying because I actually was starting to have fun working out and feared not being able to continue. I felt like I had finally found something I could do, but my body was not cooperating. My 9:30 a.m. crew all gathered around me and gave me tons of hugs and support. I went to the doctor and had an MRI performed on my knees. The MRI revealed that I have significant arthritis in both of my knees, but the left knee was described as being bone-on-bone.

I told my doctor about this amazing new program I started and how much I liked it only to have him say, "I can't tell you what to do, but if it was me, I would quit that program and maybe try yoga or something." He went on to show me pictures and explain why he felt that way. I left the office so confused, since my brain was saying listen to the doctor, but my heart was saying "No" keep on doing what you're doing. Well, I listened to my heart. I continued going every day, and I modified most of my exercises along with wearing knee braces to help. I am so excited and so happy. I stayed with The MAX program. It has only been 14 weeks to this point, and I am already able to perform most of the exercises without modification. I have dropped a couple of pant sizes, and my knee pain is nothing compared to weeks 1 through 3. In fact, I forget to wear my knee brace on occasion, because I forget about the arthritis.

The moral of my story is that this program really worked for me in so many ways. I am very thankful to my neighbor who told me about her success in the program and convinced me to give it a try. This program helped me learn how to eat healthy, how to enjoy working out, and how to live a more fulfilled life. Thank you to the staff at The MAX for my new outlook on life!

Donna Paprota

MAX Transformation story #76

> ## "It's like having a second family."
> ## *- Dan Scully*

My name is Dan and this is my story.

I am a 38 years old and recently lost my father to cancer. This is my first challenge. I have been over weight and out of shape for as long as I can remember. I have tried different diets and have lost weight only to put it right back on. My wife and her friend told me that they had joined and wanted me to join with them. The first thing I thought was, "This is going to be another waste of money". I felt that we would be into it for the first couple of weeks and then as we usually do, we would just stop and give up. I am making through this challenge and it won't stop there. I have lost inches but gained so much more. I am more confident, happier in my skin, and feel so much better. The motivation and support by all MAX ers is amazing. It's like having a second family. I am proud of the decision we made to join and our willingness to continue. Thank you MAX Challenge, you truly have shown me that I CAN do it.

Dan Scully

MAX Transformation story #77

> ## "I've taken baby steps, but they're letting me know they will not let me fall."
> ### - Michele Mathews

say the start of my story because if there's one thing I've learned here is that I will ALWAYS have a goal to achieve.

My first goal was to just join! Once I did my life changed. My friend list changed, it became larger. My family changed, they became very proud of me. My job changed, I have more energy and a better attitude to complete my day.

My instructors love the phrase "Comfort Zone". Once they here you are trying to overcome one, they find ways to push you and force you out of that zone! I've taken baby steps, but they're letting me know they will not let me fall.

There is not enough space to give you all the reasons The MAX makes me feel like a success in my own world!

I LOVE MY MAX FAMILY! THANK YOU ALL FROM THE BOTTOM OF MY HEART! <3

Michele Mathews

MAX Transformation story #78

> "The benefits of the program are endless."
> *- Terry B*

So where does one begin? I've always been active, stay involved with sports and recreational activities and I am generally not considered lazy. I am self-critical of all aspects of my life and always want better for myself and my loved ones. I'm sure that's not new, doesn't everybody secretly want that for themselves. Still no beginning? I was determined to get in shape, even if that simply meant doing something physically each day. I was a member of other gyms in the past but they never seemed to hold my attention for very long. Playing baseball or football without enough players for two teams can be boring and not hold your attention, tennis requires two to make it worthwhile, and playing golf alone can be boring, so I usually don't do the activities listed above unless there is that excitement that can hold my attention. Golf with a twosome or more is fantastic, a good tennis match is great win or lose. Membership in those other gyms were like that for me, they never held my attention very long. You get out of a gym membership what you put in so, there were not much results. I was still committed, determined to get in shape, not for anyone or anything but simply to know myself that I did it because it is the right and healthful thing to do. So last November, December 2014 time frame I started seeing Facebook posts from a friend of mine, he was talking about the MAX program in Toms River NJ. I decided to give it a try and went for a sample class. It was interesting and a great workout. I still was not convinced so I asked a lot of questions, probably too many but that's just me. Finally the manager (Stephanie) said you are overthinking it just try it out, it's only 10 weeks and if you don't like it you don't have to remain a member. I signed up in early January 2015. There were doubts early on, can I go every day to get my money's worth? Can I stay interested? Will I be tired? I guess those questions and many others will always be there for anything we do in life, this time I made a commitment to myself to forge ahead. So finally a beginning? Right around this same time unfortunately my brother was hospitalized in poor health. While visiting him and his family it became apparent that some family health issues were being passed from generation to generation. My mom had these same health issues prior to passing away I told my brother's wife that when he got out of the hospital I would talk with him about some ways to avoid these health issues. Unfortunately he passed away very suddenly. Well there is another part of the beginning, there can be no better reason to get in shape and lead a more healthy life than losing a loved one to avoidable health issues.

So now more about the MAX program. Please believe me when I tell you it was and is only the beginning. There is so much more to come with me and my journey with the MAX. I will continue with this program for the foreseeable future. The MAX program is fantastic. I have now been a part of the program for 8 months. I've been committed, I have worked out or exercised every day since January 12th. The benefits of the program are endless. There are classes scheduled conveniently throughout the day. There is a nutrition plan included to assist with a healthier lifestyle. The center is managed very effectively by Stephanie with support from a fabulous group of instructors. I have attended classes with all of the instructors at various times and they are all exceptional. Most of my journey has been spent with the 5 AM class each day. The instructor for this class is Chris. He has been so supportive and helpful to me. He has gone out of his way to find exercises and stretching routines that I can utilize throughout the day to further enhance my results. Speaking of results, they are unbelievable, I've gained endurance, lost many inches, lost 38 lbs. and most importantly set new goals to further enhance my fitness level. There is so much I could say about this program. Don't wait to start, get over there sign up and try it out. The program is fabulous.

Terry B

MAX Transformation story #79

> ## "It was/is the best decision of my life."
> ### - Gabriela Lazogue

I am a mother of 4, I manage my husband's electrical company in Union and I consider myself a lifetime MAX er.

About 3 years ago, shortly after my father passed away I became depressed and angry, taking my anger out on those I loved. I was also stressed from running a household, working on our electrical business and the impact of all we had to go through from losing my father. So my solution to coping with all of this, eat like there was no tomorrow. I did not realize that this was affecting me and my family. I've never been a large person but I've always let myself go 5 even 10 pounds but never 30 pounds. I even weighed less during my four pregnancies then I did these past few years.

Last September my mother was on a challenge of her own with a few co-workers and they decided they would all eat healthy and lose weight with whomever losing the most becoming the winner of $600.00. I started to see the difference in my mother and her willingness to change helped me think about myself and my health. I came across Maria's success story on The MAX Challenge from my Facebook feed and she looked great. Her pictures definitely did not look fake. She is also a mother and I said if she did it why can't I. Both my mother and Maria gave me the motivation I needed to work on losing the weight I've gained. I also wanted to be healthier, be at a better weight and have the best body I can before turning the age of 50. I was not able to start the September challenge but after speaking with Amy Walsh we set it up for me to start in January 2015.

It was/is the best decision of my life. I've lost 26 pounds in my first challenge and my body started to change. I would get lots of compliments from my group and some members even mentioned to me that they've voted for me at the end of the challenge. I was so excited, so motivated and saw that I can a make a difference in me, that I continued on and lost the next 7 pounds on my second challenge. People still saw a bigger change and have congratulated me and even said I have inspired them. This has made me more confident and a happier person. My goals have changed since starting. I'm now working on becoming an instructor at the MAX and I have my whole family involved in living a healthier life. The MAX has changed my life and no matter who I talk to, I always have a conversation about the MAX and how beneficial it has been for me.

Gabriela Lazogue

MAX Transformation story #80

"The MAX is really and truly a total body and mind makeover."
- Brian Howarth

I have been with the MAX of Springfield/Union since January 2015, I cannot believe the changes, both physical and mental, in such a short time. The most recognizable, my physical change, I have lost 61 pounds to date and a total of 30 inches. What makes this special to me, is 1 year ago, May 2014, I had an accident where I broke my leg and dislocated my ankle. After surgery to repair my leg and ankle with a plate and several screws, I was non weight bearing for 8 weeks. Limited in my physical activity at that point I began to gain more weight. When I could resume somewhat 'normal' activity in October of 2014 I was my heaviest ever...260 pounds. I wanted to and tried to lose weight but I just couldn't. I love food. In January I was introduced to the MAX. I thought why not give it a try. It's only 10 weeks. Well, my first day I wanted to die, I thought there is no way I can do this. I was winded just on the 5 minute warmup from Melissa my instructor. But little did I know how supportive EVERYONE, I mean EVERYONE is at the MAX. That is where the mental changes came in. I can still hear Melissa saying it takes 21 straight days to make something a habit. I thought, they can do it, why can't I. So I gave it the 21 days, then the rest of the 10 weeks, now 32 weeks later, I can't imagine a morning without my 5AMers

I still have pain in leg and ankle from time to time but I know it is ok to modify my workout at that time. As long as I'm doing something. I have changed into a morning person. I have become more aware of what I eat and how it affects me. I have changed my food shopping habits. I have changed my wardrobe.

The MAX is really and truly a total body and mind makeover. It has made a lasting impression on me. In July I completed my first Spartan Sprint and am in the process of signing up for another. I cannot thank the MAX trainers and staff or my fellow MAX ers enough.

Brian Howarth

MAX Transformation story #81

> ## "MAX has changed my outlook on life and what I could do."
> ### - Kathy Edmonds

My name is Kathy Edmonds and I am 44 year old woman. I never did much exercise in my life. I was always a slim person with a fairly high metabolism so there wasn't a need for it. Growing up, it wasn't something that my family ever did. Once I had my Second child I felt like I should exercise. So I joined the gym. I could never really get into it.

At the age of 26, I was diagnosed with multiple sclerosis. Because of that I didn't think I could to any strenuous activity. I did gentle yoga for a while but that's about it. My coworker and friend Christine Barker joined MAX about a year and a half ago. She achieved amazing results. She asked me numerous times to come to a class to see what it's like and I always thought there is no way that I could do that. It wasn't just the exercise but the nutrition as well. I have two boys 9 and 13 and both can be finicky eaters at times. I thought to myself - how can I give up dairy, how can I give up bread?

At the end of the school year we had a health fair that the teachers were required to go to. It had many vendors from our health insurance company to local vendors sharing information with us. MAX was one of those vendors. A coworker brought me over to the MAX table. Stacy has been going to MAX for about a year. I was told there was a sample class coming up. I said I would go even though in my mind I was thinking of all the reasons why I couldn't. A lot of them had to do with what I thought was my limited abilities because of MS.

I went to the first class which was led by Natalie Burke - an amazing woman - and I was hooked! I was a little apprehensive with the nutrition piece but my husband was incredibly supportive. He knew this would be something that would be great for my health. Having the support of my husband helped tremendously.

With MAX, I loved being part of a group where everyone was working towards the same goal. Everyone was so supportive and helpful. My instructor Natalie Burke is amazing. She came to my house after the first week of classes to show me modifications that I could do so that I could be part of the exercises that were happening in class.

9 weeks later and I have gotten incredibly strong and can do things that I never thought I could do before.

MAX has changed my outlook on life and what I could do. Having MS can go hand-in-hand with depression. I know I have suffered from that in the past. MAX has change my mind set and increased my confidence a thousand fold. It also taught me how to eat in a nutritious, healthy way. A side bonus of this is that my children see the success I have had. It's rubbing off on them. They are interested in healthy eating as well as exercise. It is a bonus I could never have imagined happening. I feel so lucky to have gone to the first introductory class. I can't wait to continue on as a legacy member and see how much more I can progress!

Kathy Edmonds

MAX Transformation story #82

> **"Thank you MAX for changing my eating habits and creating a healthy way of eating and living!"**
> *- Kim Wade*

I had my first introduction to MAX through a friend last year. Even after seeing her great results, I was still a bit skeptical about the program, thinking it probably wouldn't work for me – just another fad diet that is unmaintainable. I ended up winning a 10 week membership in March through a charity event and thought I had nothing to lose in giving the program a try. I made it to class 5 days a week for the entire challenge, only missing one class and followed the nutrition the best that I could (I actually found it difficult to eat so much food – especially in the first stage). I honestly was incredibly surprised at my before/after pics for 2 reasons: first, I didn't realize I had gotten so heavy in the first place, and secondly, during the entire challenge, I didn't feel I was achieving results. When I was shown my after pic, I was incredibly pleased with the transformation via picture & even more so when the announced me as the $1000 winner of the challenge! I lost a total of 14 inches and 26 pounds. I just completed my 2nd challenge, losing another 8 inches and 10 pounds following the legacy program stage 4 not eating carbs (but not cycling fruit carbs or fats). My waist size alone has gone down 10 inches! I have nothing but amazing praises to say to all involved at the MAX, from the friendly faces going through the same daily challenges as myself, to the coaches, online support groups, and those involved in creating the program. As one can clearly see through before and after pictures alone, the program works – the pictures are not modified or air brushed and are from a 10 week span.

Thank you MAX for changing my eating habits and creating a healthy way of eating and living!

Kim Wade

MAX Transformation story #83

Kim Wade, MAX Transformation story #83 – Before and After picture

"MAX is a family... A family I could never imagine not having in my life"
- Francine Miraglia

Hi!! My name is Francine, I am 39 years old and I am an Old Bridge MAX er!

My story starts back in 1983, when I was 8 years old!! I was a very chubby child. I struggled with my weight my entire adolescence. I would go to Weight Watchers with my dad at 12 years old!!! I was the youngest person there... It sucked! In 1998, at 22 years old, I hired a personal trainer to get me in "Wedding shape"... And I succeeded! I was at my ideal weight! Over the next few years I struggled with trying to conceive a child. My body was being riddled with hormones to help me! The weight just started to creep back on. After 2 miscarriages and 9 fertility procedures, I finally welcomed 2 boys in 2003 and 2005. The stress of motherhood, and being home every day was too much to bare. I just ate and ate and ate!! I was nearly 300 lbs.! I was so depressed that I thought my only answer was to have another baby. So now I had to endure more drugs and more procedures. But this time the outcome wasn't good. I lost my son nearly halfway through my pregnancy. I blamed myself and my obesity! So in 2010 I started exercising and I found a doctor who would give me a magic pill... I lost 80 lbs... I was thrilled! So happy that apparently life gave me a gift... On my own I conceived my son, who is now 3 1/2 years old. Over the last 3 years I went back to my old habits... Eating and not moving my butt off the couch! I was miserable yet again... And gained all 80 lbs. back! Over the last 2 years I had been hearing about MAX ... I drove past it every day. I wondered..... Could I do it? Would I be embarrassed? Would I fail? Well the answer to those questions is YES I could do it! NO I won't be embarrassed or fail!! On June 29, 2015 I signed up for my first challenge. I was petrified! But I bought my containers, I cooked my food, and I went to class!! I did things I never ever thought I would do. I also never missed a Monday! For me that was huge. I followed the nutrition almost perfectly, I enjoyed my treat meals and most of all I actually really like to exercise! I still can't believe that I can say that out loud!! This challenge I lost 25lbs and inches all over! My husband and my boys have been wonderful and supportive and I truly couldn't have done this without their love and support. Finally, my MAX story would be incomplete without mentioning the AMAZING support system at Old Bridge. The staff, trainers and coaches are the absolute best! They pushed me further than I ever thought possible. The friends I have made over the last 11 weeks will most likely be the best friends I will ever have in my life. I have signed up for Legacy and I am continuing on my journey to find good health and happiness! I turn 40 in 9 weeks... My new life is just starting!! MAX is a family... A family I could never imagine not having in my life.... A very important part of my story!

Francine Miraglia

MAX Transformation story #84

"I hit a plateau and realized I needed a place where I could train but also one that was fully committed to NUTRITION."
- Ivona Qualy

Over the past four years, I have gone way outside my comfort zone doing 5Ks, triathlons, tough mudders, long distance cycling and running, and last year my first half marathon.

When I started in 2011, I was terribly unfit and over-weight. Training for these races helped build my strength and endurance. In 2013, I hit a plateau and realized I needed a place where I could train but also one that was fully committed to NUTRITION. This is how I found Stephanie Monninger Franolich and the MAX of Toms River. Since I walked through their doors, I have set new personal records, broke through my plateau, toned and conditioned my body, increased my endurance, and I have been off thyroid meds for 12 months.

Thank you MAX of Toms River ... You all have given me a great place to train hard, to sweat and to push my limits!!! Xoxoxo

Ivona Qualy

MAX Transformation story #85

Ivona Qualy, MAX Transformation story #85 – Before and After picture

> "I believe the MAX can help me stay alive and
> physically fit for the next 40."
> - *Bob Brennan*

I joined the MAX after seeing my friends before and after picture upon completing his first MAX Challenge. Coincidently, this took place upon my return from the mall. I was shopping for a bigger pair of pants. I had a little bit of a melt down and I never bought the bigger pants, I just left feeling disgusted. I was using my bout with cancer as a sort of excuse for letting myself go. There should be no excuse. This event took place on a Saturday. I signed up for my first challenge on Sunday and attended class on Monday.

My first class was rough and I wound up throwing up, not on anyone, I did that in private. I was in a class with a bunch of strangers who had the same deer in the headlights look on their faces. Most of the class was women. We were given the literature about nutrition and given advice on how and what to eat. For the first half of the challenge I was constantly thinking "I need to do something manly", I am not saying that the work outs were easy, I was hurting. There was a lot of hopping and jumping and I am as graceful as an Ox, I was out of my comfort zone. I "though" that I needed to be doing Cross Fit or something with Mixed Martial Arts or kick boxing.

One day, in the middle of class, a light bulb went on in my head. The ladies in my class had every bit as much heart and soul, determination and spirit as some of the Marines that I had served with. Granted, I wouldn't take the ladies into a fire fight, but they had guts and I admire guts. It came to me, I am where I am supposed to be, these are my people and

I appreciate everyone that sets foot in this arena to become a better version of their former self. I have been motivated and inspired by my classmates throughout this journey. The smiling, sweaty, red faces and high fives speak to my soul.

I am 48 years old. I have spent the first 40 years trying to kill myself in one way or another. I believe the MAX can help me stay alive and physically fit for the next 40. I am motivated to keep going. I look forward to inspiring others in their challenges and I hope that someday, I can encourage and motivate someone in the same way my friends pictured moved me. I have recently been hired as a trainer for the MAX of Morristown and I have been training and teaching under the Supervision of Toby in Montclair.

Bob Brennan

MAX Transformation story #86

"I'm so glad that I stuck with the program."
- Melissa K

Everyone starts at different points. Everyone has their own goals. And everyone's journey moves at a different pace.

For me, the MAX Challenge was perfect. 10 weeks, 50 classes of high intensity interval training. A chance to build muscle, lose fat and get personal training along the way. If that didn't inspire me enough, a nutrition program full of nutrition dense foods and a treat meal every week! Did I mention an amazing group of supportive and non-judgmental people?

Week 1, I remember that I couldn't even hold a modified plank for a minute. Robots and mountain climbers... I had zero coordination to do them too. It was tough but I enjoyed the challenge. After phase 1, I had already lost 7 lbs. so that gave me such motivation.

Around week 5, I hit a rough patch: the scale stopped moving and a friend told me "I should weigh less than I do". It really hurt. I stuck with the nutrition for the most part and went to class but stopped pushing myself hard. I was ready to quit. I finally spoke to my trainer and a few others at the MAX, and they were so helpful and supportive. I finally got out of my rut and really started pushing myself again. I was able to hold a plank for 3 minutes with excellent form. I'm so glad that I stuck with the program.

At the end of 10 weeks, I lost 11 lbs. But more importantly, I lost 10 inches total! If it's one thing I learned, the scale means nothing. It doesn't tell you fat vs muscle. The MAX is more than weight loss... it's gaining muscle and strength, appreciating the body you have and learning a healthy lifestyle that you can share with everyone in your life!

Melissa K

MAX Transformation story #87

Melissa K, MAX Transformation story #87 – Before and After picture

"Yes, I confess I am a MAX Addict and proudly admit it!"
- Linda Perry

I have had my diet battles since puberty. 4 years ago, I successfully lost 67 pounds in 10 months through diet and it started creeping back. Though not a stress eater, stress definitely affects my metabolism and realizing that was one of the factors in deciding to try The MAX Challenge. Other reasons involved my sister having a stroke right after her 56th birthday with NO family history and also being told that I have arthritis in my hip. I needed to lose some weight but also incorporate some exercise this time - so after much contemplation, I joined MAX.

My first week, I was Gung Ho. I could do this - easy. The second week, I was questioning my sanity. I must be crazy to be doing this. But I signed up for 10 weeks and I am not a quitter. So I gave myself "goals". Let's make it to 20% done, 25%, etc. when I hit 50%, it made no sense to NOT finish. I was starting to feel and see the difference, even if no one else was yet. I was also starting to feel like family. No one judges anyone, they encourage each other. By the 9th week, I realized due to scheduling conflicts for the summer, that I would need to take a break and I was actually TORN about it. Oh my God, I became a MAX Addict and there is no available rehab program for it! The 10th week convinced me that I did the right thing by signing up. Why? Because even though I know you are supposed to throw out your scale, I did not and am glad I did not. I lost 25 pounds and almost 15 inches overall in 10 weeks!

So, even though I took the summer off, I stayed with the nutrition for much of it (I admit to not being totally compliant on vacation, though I did try somewhat - and my birthday became a treat day, not a treat meal) but I am aware I did that and put myself on track again. I did exercises as best I could, despite a neck injury. I am starting my first round of Legacy in a few days and am looking forward to being with my "family" again!

Linda Perry

MAX Transformation story #88

> ### "Everyone there is inspiring to me."
> ### *- Joanie Daugherty*

The MAX, the MAX is everything to me. The only other gyms I went to were ones that I could work out solo, classes were not my thing as I did not feel I would be able to keep up or would look like a total spaz.

A year before I started the MAX was a very tough year. The police had come to my door to notify me that my ex-husband and father of my 8 year old was found dead in his apartment. My 22 year old who loved him as a father was also deeply affected. Shortly after this I was diagnosed with Melanoma Stage 1 in my neck and it was removed and was cleared. My car which was paid off was totaled but thankfully no one was hurt. I then had a precancerous mole removed from the back of my leg and it became infected because the stiches would not keep it closed. LONG story short I ended up with a hole behind my knee in the crease where you bend and was erroneously put on bed rest with no activity and plummeted into a dark hole which I never experienced before. I spent 3 months essentially in my room trying to still run a house and for the first time in my life was out of work on disability. I received Iodine washings and the wound began to heal. It healed wrong and had to be reopened and then packed and unpacked twice a day for over 2 months. My roommate is a Saint and would have tears in her eyes doing this. I was in so much pain and would turn the music up and send my Juliet into the other side of the house so she would not hear me scream.

I eventually got better physically, but I was the heaviest I had ever been. My mother noticed and said something at least once a week. I went back to work and continued to eat badly as though I did not care. My daughter's friend Kass told me about the MAX and I thought about it and didn't go. Then my friend Adrienne told me she was going and the excitement she expressed about the program clicked and I came and have been coming ever since. The only times I have missed is when I have a work schedule I cannot adjust or have been ill. I did not follow the nutrition to a T but I plan on doing so with the next challenge. My family has been eating better and I have made better choices and am more conscious of what I eat. I feel 100% better than I did and have come a long way with what I can do now and compared to what I could not do when I started. I have the bad habit of weighing myself every day but have seen the results mostly in the clothes in my closet that now fit. Just this summer I was going to buy a bathing suit and my roommate reminded me of the one she bought me last year. I told her it would never fit as I could not even pull it over my shoulders last year. She said try it just for fun. I did, and it fit!!!! It is too big now!!!!! I want to run a 5K and I am looking to replace my old bike. I no longer get out of breathe bringing the laundry up the stairs. I am still working on strengthening my legs as I think the bed rest I was on adversely affected them.

The biggest transition I noticed was when I was trying to find a before picture. That was hard. I am the one who hides behind my kids in pictures, just showing my face or I am the one taking the pictures. I have plenty of pictures for after because my smile is bright and I am standing next to people and I am even in a bathing suit in some!!! But truly the best compliment I received was the first day of school for Juliet. I was walking into the school alone as Juliet was already inside and the secretary was holding the door waiting for me. I had my gym clothes on and no make-up, I thought I was a wreck. She is giving me this peculiar look, then she suddenly smiles and says Oh My God I didn't recognize you, you lost a lot of weight!!! I actually gave her a hug!! I am surprised people even notice because I see how successful others at the MAX have been and do not think the change in me is as drastic as theirs. Everyone there is inspiring to me. The trainer's personalities are infectious and their energy truly contagious. I have tried another MAX due to work schedule but found none compare to the staff at the Toms River MAX. They feel like family and I feel like I belong and my successes are theirs too. It is not just physical for me but it is amazing what is has done for my mental health. It is ME time and time I do not feel guilty for taking!!

Joanie Daugherty

MAX Transformation story #89

"I went from standing in the back to moving up to the front of the room."
- Kelly Niro

Twenty weeks ago I found myself in the worst funk of my life! I was carrying extra pounds that made me feel self-conscious and unattractive. All my life, I have been tall and thin, I never had to diet let alone exercise. The loss of my mother and brother took its toll on me emotionally, my father became very ill which the little time I had to go to the gym stopped right away, the stress caused me to become less active. I was tired of the muffin top and its constant battle of trying to hide it. I'm 46 years old and I was beginning to feel depressed. I knew I needed to get "ME" back, I AM a beautiful woman, and I had to stop feeling sorry for myself because no one can do this but ME!

I was told about The MAX and its program and my immediate thought was, I can't walk in there and do that! It's totally out of my comfort zone, I am no way shape or form coordinated, more like a fish out of water! Seriously, the thought of walking in the door made me sick to my stomach. After thinking about it, I decided to try the sample class. Oh my gosh, I LOVED IT!!! I was so excited about it, I joined that day and I was ready for the next challenge! I walked in the doors Monday - Friday leaving everything that was negative and holding me back outside, this was MY time, this is where it was all about ME, all my energy was focused on changing me from the inside out! I gave it my all everyday huffing and puffing, leaving puddles of sweat on the mat was a daily occurrence. I did have an issue with my knee, it was holding me back, it was reminding me that I needed to get it looked at. I went to the Doctor, he recommended physical therapy, I looked at him, and he asked that I give it a couple of weeks. I didn't have time for that, my challenge just started, I gave myself 2 weeks, made an appointment at 8:30 before my class and asked for a shot, I knew it would work and I would be back on track. I told my doctor what this meant to me and I had 10 weeks in order to prove to myself that YES, I could take a leap out of my comfort zone and survive! The shot worked and I was giving a 110%, I noticed my waist getting smaller, my stomach going down and the holes in my belt were getting tighter. The excitement I felt with my body changing was incredible, my 9:30 MAX crew and instructor Stephanie were so supportive, we were each other's cheerleaders! The exercises I have done in class I would have never thought I could do, I am so much stronger and healthier! My family has also become healthier because of my lifestyle change.

I finished my FIRST 10 week challenge with the biggest smile on my face, I knew I was going to have amazing results, I lost 22 pounds and 18 1/4 inches! I was beyond thrilled, I DID IT! I worked hard every day, there were days I amazed myself and yelled out I finally did it!!! My MAX family voted for me as a finalist for my class for the greatest transformation, I have to say it touched me beyond words, ME? Really? Our kick off meeting, it was announced that...... I WON THE GREATEST TRANSFORMATION! Who would have thought the girl who was afraid to walk through the doors and hid in the back of the room would be recognized for all my hard work and dedication? THE MAX OF TOMS RIVER DID!!!

I went from standing in the back to moving up to the front of the room. I am no longer afraid of the unknown, I am so confident, stronger and healthier. I walk in the doors onto the mats and I continue to give it my all! I am obsessed with The MAX and what the program has taught me, I am a healthier, happier more confident woman!

Kelly Niro

MAX Transformation story #90

Kelly Niro, MAX Transformation story #90 – Before and After picture

> "When I started this journey I never imagined I
> would be where I am today."
> *- Christine Cracchiolo*

MAY 2014

Today I broke through barriers (boards) a time to reflect where we were, where we are and where we are going, and tomorrow I celebrate my 1 year MAXiversary. When I started this journey I never imagined I would be where I am today. I never imagined gaining anything except some aches and pains and more weight when I fell off the program. To my delightful surprise I have gained so much from this amazing group of people I have come to know. I have gained a family of sincere, honest, caring people who give me strength, confidence, support, validation, recognition, and smiles every day. I have learned that I can do whatever I put my heart, mind and soul to and when I am struggling, I have an amazing group of people to help me achieve my goal. I am not perfect and have struggles week to week. Some days I just can't get motivated or just feel blah. I have learned through this program that it's okay. Tomorrow is a new day, leave yesterday behind. I never imagined that I would inspire people other than maybe my kids or that someone would be interested in my story, or that I would be asked to be a coach/mentor or to have people that you know and some you don't, message you or stop you when you're out to tell you that you inspire them or motivate them and you are the reason they are working out or eating healthy, it is an emotional experience, heartwarming and just pushes me harder to continue my journey. I started MAX at 223 lbs., a size 18/20 Today I weigh 158 and I wear a size 10/12. My 1st day at MAX I couldn't even do 1 jumping jack. I barely got my feet of the ground. By day 3, I was done. I sat on my couch asking why am I doing this to myself, I could not move my arms I was so sore. MY WHY was staring right at me, pictures of my family? I continue with my struggles and challenges everyday but I now do this for me first. I want to be healthy and strong in mind, body and spirit. This program has given me that and I am so honored, humbled and blessed to be able to be a part of MAX everyday thanks to Rich Bruno and Evan Hadzimichalis, If not for your support, kindness, spirit and confidence in me I wouldn't be here today. To Katie Normandia your shout outs every morning encourage me to keep going. Priscilla Maiko McRae, Allison Gaynor Palace although I am not in your class you are always there with positive words, smiles and encouragement. To my 6 am MAX ers you all hold a special place in my heart, your high fives and motivation every morning inspire me to be the best that I can be. To the 5 am crew, bless you all for your devotion and motivation to MAX. Seeing you finish your workout every morning with such sweat and dedication inspires me. To my fellow FB MAX ers your knowledge, struggles and triumphs that you share with us every day are a source of comfort, it proves where not alone and we all have our own stuff. Keep sharing your stories they change people's attitude one by one. There is so much more I could say but most importantly thank you Bryan Klein for having the vision to change people's lives from the inside out. A few final words to my husband Joseph Cracchiolo, I couldn't do this without your love and support and to my daughters, Stefani Cracchiolo, Brooke Cracchiolo and Karina... you are my true inspirations and I continue with this journey so I can live a long life with you and to show you working hard at something is truly rewarding.

Christine Cracchiolo

MAX Transformation story #91

"Everyone is so nonjudgmental and helpful, especially to the newbies."
- Meg Mendelson

In January 2013 my son, Seth, joined The MAX. He was the winner of his class for that challenge and made major changes to his body. The next challenge my daughter, Caitlin, joined and had great results for herself too. The next challenge, my husband, Rubin, joined. He went on to lose 90 lbs. over the first year and has kept it off since. I would cook for them according to the MAX meal plan, keeping track of their carb and no carb days. I'd wave goodbye to them when they left for their class. Everyone would ask me, when are YOU joining? I would respond, "NEVER". I had no desire to go to a class at 8:30 pm five nights a week when I had to get up at 6 am for work every day. I liked my quiet nights at home. I wasn't overweight. Etc.

In January 2014, I was diagnosed with breast cancer. I went through chemotherapy for 5 months and then radiation. In the fall when chemo was finished, I said to my oncologist, what is your best advice to me on how to prevent this cancer from recurring? She said to watch your diet and exercise 4-5 days a week. Hmmmm interesting but no light bulb went off. I just figured I'd join a box gym. One day. A few months later, Rubin and I downsized to a new home. I was walking our dogs the first day and suddenly realized that with this move, I could start some new routines. Usually when Rubin went to the gym, I'd wave goodbye to him from my computer. An hour later when he returned, there I'd be, still on the computer. I came inside and told him that I was thinking of joining The MAX. He was totally shocked. My kids were shocked. I think I was in shock too, but it just felt right.

I started in March 2015. After not really being an "exercise person" I was over zealous and thought I could do jumping jacks like I was in grade school again. Subsequently I had some initial aches and pains, but I got through it by modifying. I came to find out that they were right all along: this MAX thing IS really fun!! Who would think that going to a gym class with a bunch of strangers could make you laugh. And those strangers have turned into friends. Everyone is so nonjudgmental and helpful, especially to the newbies. My health is the number one reason I joined the MAX and have continued to go.

Meg Mendelson

MAX Transformation story #92

"Thank you all so much for restoring my HOPE"
- Nessa Mitchell

Three weeks before joining MAX - I went shopping at Lane Bryant - At the time I wore a size 22 but I bought clothes in sizes 24-26 and 3x-4X. Why?? because I gave up all hope of ever losing weight - I figured since nothing had worked in the past - I should just be prepared for when I gained more weight - I figured it would only be a short time before I was in the larger sizes - see I had tried EVERYTHING to lose weight - Weight Watchers, Jenny Craig, Nutri System, Surgery, ...Pills, Starvation, Liquids, Acupuncture, the list goes on. And nothing worked - I joined gyms, did Zumba - bought a treadmill etc.

It wasn't until I met Lee Grebler , Elissa Scheer Grebler, Sean O'Halpin and the 6am Group that I started to believe in the "impossible" again - Everything that they told me was true - Everything that they said would happen, actually happened - I feel great, I am looking better, and am succeeding at weight loss FINALLY -

I just completed 10 weeks and I am now wearing a size 16. And as for all those clothes I purchased :) they have all been returned :)

Thank you all so much for restoring my HOPE

Nessa Mitchell

MAX Transformation story #93

> **"I was asked to write down my goals the only thing that came to mind was don't throw up during class or have them take the defibrillator off the wall"**
> *- Cathy Vincent*

was 3 months shy of turning 50 when I decided to join MAX. I saw the mailings that were sent to my office and was interested in this 10 week challenge. When I went to the kick-off I was asked to write down my goals the only thing that came to mind was don't throw up during class or have them take the defibrillator off the wall. I did think it would be nice to fit in those old clothes I've been hanging on to. Other than my immediate family, I didn't tell anyone I was doing MAX. This way if I gave up I didn't have to share my failure with others. On March 30, 2015, I walked through the doors of MAX and the Owner, instructors, and members were all so welcoming. Workouts were tough in the beginning. After the doing 10 jumping jacks in warm ups I winded and I thought maybe I was too old for this type of workout. What was I thinking? But I modified the exercises and kept pushing through. My instructor, Kelly, kept reminding us to give it your all for 10 weeks, just 10 weeks, you will see results. Because I was told nutrition was 80% of the program, I would say I was 90% compliant. I say 10% non-compliant because I didn't read labels as well as I do now and some things slipped by. I took pictures and measurements when I first started. If I felt weight wasn't coming off, I would do a measurement and see ½ to 1 inch come off. At least I knew my hard work was doing something. Then people started to notice and asked what I was doing. I realized this program was really working and shared my success story with them. I finished my first challenge down 26 lbs. and went from a size 14 to a 10. After my second challenge, I'm down 39 lbs. and in a loose size

8. I haven't worn a size 8 in 25 years. There are so many inspiring people at MAX who helped me get where I am today. It's an amazing feeling and I have everyone at MAX to thank for that.

Cathy Vincent

MAX Transformation story #94

"It happened so gradually, it just seemed almost natural to be a big, heavy guy. But, I needed a change. How had I gained nearly 100 pounds??"
- Doug Dreger

This past Memorial Day 2014, the numbers 2-7-0 stared up at me from my bathroom scale, as I walked out the door and went to my first class at MAX of Woodbridge.

As a teen and young adult, I had been one of those absurdly fit, naturally athletic types. Always a starter on the high school track and volleyball teams, always active, with a metabolism that would not quit. At about six feet tall, I weighed 175 dripping wet.

Funny how 25 years of inactivity at a desk job, and a penchant for fast food, changed all that. Slowly, so slowly, I just got fat and lazy. It happened so gradually, it just seemed almost natural to be a big, heavy guy. But, I needed a change. How had I gained nearly 100 pounds?? My wife and I had a new baby now, and I was 46 years old. I had to make a change and get healthy for them.

I've lost 52 pounds since that 1st day of my MAX experience. 52 pounds in 14 weeks, and my waist is 6 inches smaller!

If anyone needed proof that this program works, that the nutrition plan is sound, and the trainers are AWESOME, results like this should tell the story.

After these 14 weeks, including my first 10-week challenge, I'm stronger, faster, and excited to keep going strong!

I cannot thank the MAX WB team enough for their support and motivation.

Doug Dreger

MAX Transformation story #95

> ## "I felt stronger, more energized, more confident, and more ALIVE."
> ### - Stephanie Vicidomini

I will never forget the phone call that forever changed my life. I was just calling to ask a few questions about this program that everyone was talking about. I never knew that on the other end of the phone would be one of my biggest supporters, cheerleaders and motivators just a few short weeks later. While on the phone I expressed all my fears, my reasons why it can't work, my sicknesses, and insecurities. Wendy just sat there and listened. She listened to me cry, stating how last year I went to look into the weight loss surgery and backed out. How all I want is to feel healthy so that I can get pregnant. How my weight gain in the last 10 years holds me back from everything. That day Wendy promised me that if I gave my all, and committed that together we could make it a success. I agreed to give it a shot. We hung up and a few minutes later my phone rang. Wendy was on the other line in tears, she told me she understood how I felt and that she wanted to truly help me reach my goal and prove to myself that I could do this. I was in awe that she cared so much, at that time she didn't even know who I was. From that day forward, Wendy continued to call, text, and Facebook message me and encourage me in class. She made me feel strong when I felt weak. She never let me down, and even when I wanted to give up I knew that I made that promise to her to keep going. I can proudly say that within a few weeks I felt so many small changes in my body. I felt stronger, more energized, more confident, and more ALIVE. Something I haven't felt in years. About 3 weeks later I could touch my toes for the first time ever. A few weeks after that I could do pushups, sit ups and hold a plank. Here I am about to enter into my second challenge and I look back at all the times I said I CAN'T and now say I CAN. I was able to do things like, line dance something I LOVE, but couldn't do because I would be so out of breath. I signed up for my first 5 K and will be doing it this weekend, again something I always wanted to do but never could. I lost 25 lbs. and went down 4 dress sizes. But most of all I found my inner strength. I found my fight. Without Wendy, Mario and Jen at the Cranford MAX my life would be completely different. I am so thankful I picked up the phone that day and I hope they know how amazing my life is now because of them. Thank you doesn't seem like enough for everything I have gained.

Stephanie Vicidomini

MAX Transformation story #96

This is how is all begins. Being a single mom I never thought about me until now. Sure I was unhappy with me but now I know it was my inner Soul plus of course my body was not twiggy. That's was our role model growing up in the 70's. One day my 4 year old grandchild said "Grammy you are squishy". Wow - I looked at myself in the mirror for the first time in a long while and said JULIANNA you are right. You have a squishy grandma. A few weeks past and I find myself in Point Pleasant celebrating my 7 year old grand child's birthday. My daughter's sister in-law was there but she looked awesome. Thinner and happy so of course I ask the question how did you do it. She lost inches and 38 pounds as she proudly explains her journey. She says The MAX Challenge changed her life. She also tells me she won the Staten Island MAX Challenge. So inspiring she was so I go on my iPhone and Google the closest MAX to my home which was Montclair. So now my journey begins, I filled out the form and I get an immediate response from a Toby. I keep telling Toby all excuses - so am I really ready. Toby just kept sending me messages so I finally call. I have been involved with many gyms but did they care about me. I wanted them to know if I was there. I asked Toby how you know if I am there and her quick wonderful response was "the only reason for you not to be here is if you have a broken leg". That was it I wanted it!!! Toby cares! She changes lives one person at a time. I am a missionary and will be traveling to Haiti. I am changed physically and spiritually. Toby is our treasure that is shared to all of the amazing MAX community. I am truly changing my mind, body and soul. Thank you thank you thank you. Warmly. This is my life and I am the happiest I have ever been.

Cathy Marto

MAX Transformation story #97

> *"I now have the tools to continue as a Legacy member and I now know what the future holds."*
> *- Kathy Z*

first heard about the MAX Challenge from some friends on Facebook and some family members and all of them had great success with the program. My first impression was "wow that sounds really hard to do". Both the friends and the family members lived far from me so it never crossed my mind to join. I have been somewhat overweight ever since grammar school. I was always trying to lose weight, eat right, and exercise, but just couldn't get it right. I was looking for help but how could I exercise 5 days a week and eat the way they were eating? I hated exercise and had every excuse not to do it. Summer was here and I still didn't' lose the weight I wanted to. I had tried all winter but could barely lose 5 pounds.

Then one Saturday morning I was on Facebook and an end of the challenge pictures of my friend and decided to look online and see if there were any centers by me. The Montclair MAX popped up and I said to myself "let me fill out the form and see what happens". Toby, the owner of the Montclair MAX called me back within 5 minutes. She explained the program to me and for every excuse I gave her as to my schedule conflicts, physical limitations, and my complaints about exercise she assured me that I could do it despite all that. She made me feel so comfortable from the first minute I spoke to her and made me feel like it was a program that would work for me. I spoke to my husband and asked him if he would like join and he said yes which made it even better. Now her site did not open for three weeks so for three weeks that is all I thought about. We signed up for 5 am class as that was the best time for both of us to go together and it haunted me all that time. How was I ever going to get up at 4:30 in the morning to exercise and follow the nutrition, let alone during the summer? Well 10 weeks have passed; we attended 40 out of the 50 classes and only missed them due to vacation. I have never workout 40 days in a 6 month period let alone 10 weeks. I lost 14 pounds and 15 inches and that may not look like a lot but what you can't see is how much stronger I have become physically doing exercises I never thought I could do.   What you can't see how my attitude toward exercise and eating better has changed. What you can't see is how this program makes me pop out of bed in the morning at 4:40 am each day because I know that after I finish that 45 minutes of exercise I am done with my workout. I don't feel guilty that I didn't exercise after work. I now have the tools to continue as a Legacy member and I now know what the future holds.

Now how did we do it? We did it with the support from the MAX family which it truly is a family. This program has more support than any program I have ever tried and I have tried them all throughout my life. It is a combination of exercise and nutrition but most of all it is from the support of Toby, the trainers, the other members in my class and Facebook. They make the class fun. The 45 minute class is just enough to get a great workout but not too long where you can't physically do it anymore. The class keeps you moving from one exercise to another and you don't get bored. If an exercise gets too hard you know in 30 or 60 seconds you will be moving onto something else so you keep going. Every day and each week is different which makes it fun and keeps you going and makes you not want to miss a class. As the weeks go by you start to see results in the way you feel, the way your cloths fit, and the way you think and how others see you. After 10 weeks of pushing yourself and being pushed by others you will get better and better at the exercises and the nutrition. The Team spirit that we have also keeps us going. Everyone wants to help each other and cheer each other on. All of this makes you feel and know that you can do it and we are not alone. With all that said I am not perfect at this and don't know that I will ever be. As long as I keep trying to learn the nutrition and challenge myself each day with the exercise I know I will keep seeing results. I like that the program is 10 weeks and after that you get to start all over again. It is a great way to keep us motivated and have fresh start. We learn what we didn't do right the first round and keep doing what we did well.

I truly love this program and would recommend it to everyone. The positive team environment is something I have never experience before. It definitely works. There are measurable results for everyone whether we can see them or not.   Now that I have seen all the before and after pictures from this last challenge I don't think there is a single person that did not benefit from this program in one way or another. I know people are stronger then when they started. I know people lost weight, inches, and made their bodies stronger. Other changes are happening too on the inside not only by lowering blood pressure, cholesterol, sugar etc. but also in our minds. We are removing the negative thoughts of "I can't do this to "yes I can do this" and we look forward to what's next. I think we all have our own challenges and come to the program from a different prospective but once you get here, with the MAX, we are all in it together.

I want to thank Toby, the owner of the Montclair MAX. She made what seemed was so out of our reach to something that we accomplished together and could not have done it without her support. Thanks so much to Sarah, Bob and Jeannis and the 5 am crew and yes I still go at 5 am. I want to especially thank my husband the most for his 24 hour support through this journey and looking forward to being legacy members and continue our journey together. I am so thankful I found the MAX. It was the answer I have been looking for my whole life.

Kathy Z

MAX Transformation story #98

Kathy Z, MAX Transformation story #98 – Before and After picture

"I had gained 50 pounds that I desperately wanted to lose but I had lost my vitality and drive."
- Sandra Soehngen

I am turning 60. Two years ago I had both of my hips replaced. The decision to have hip surgery was after 10 years of chronic hip pain which had escalated to such an intensity that simply walking created unbearable pain. Of course my weight increased every year with my dwindling activity and then add to that my body's change from menopause.

I had gained 50 pounds that I desperately wanted to lose but I had lost my vitality and drive.

How do you shed the weight and inches that get packed on to your body from 10+ years of neglect and over eating? I'd join a gym, go on a diet, fast, try to be more active but I'd always lose give up and return to old habits. Then the weight would come back and the fatalism that this was who I had become and would be forever more.

I felt old, weak, fat, tired and DEPRESSED!

Then I saw it, an ad in a local magazine about a 10 week program called The MAX Challenge and it was so close to where I live I thought how could I not try it. Plus there was a picture of someone with a before and after. Not a model with a touched up photo but someone real. I made the call, spoke with Toby told her my story, my concern about my hips. Toby assured me there are modifications that she would show me so I wouldn't hurt myself or risk dislocating my bionic hips.

I remember that first class... jumping jacks (I think I could only do 2), pushups, planks, abs, sit ups it didn't stop for 45 minutes and all I could think of was "you've got to be kidding". Thought I would never be able to do any of it. My face beet red and panting, sweating like I NEVER sweat before in any dance class, spin class, yoga class or any place else. But this time I stayed the course, showed up every morning 6AM and every day I got stronger and fitter.

After the first 10 week challenge my waist went down 6 inches! My hips 4 inches and I'm not stopping there. I haven't felt this young and strong since I can't even remember. But the best part is the friends I have made and the privilege of being a witness to their transformations too.

One of the most important elements of The MAX Challenge is the community of likeminded people (women and men) who have this common goal - transformation. Watching everyone drop pounds and smile more is my daily inspiration. Took me ten years to put the weight on, it will take some time and SWEAT to take it off. I'm willing to stay the course with my MAX buddies to achieve it. (PS - I am doing a lot of cooking too.) The MAX of Montclair is a great place to grow and lose that fat that has been hanging on and won't go away. Thank you Toby Wachstein

Sandra Soehngen

MAX Transformation story #99

> "It's not just a gym or a fitness class or a diet. It's a way of life."
> *- Norma Callahan*

I started this year off the heaviest I've ever been. I was feeling very depressed and hopeless. To top it off my father was in very poor health and I feared that I may lose him. By Feb., my father miraculously got better. Seeing him better than I've ever seen him before, he gave me the inspiration and motivation to better myself.

In March, as I looked at the local paper/Marketeer, I saw the MAX Challenge flyer and made the call.......several times. I started March 30, 2015. I'm glad I did, it's the best thing I've done for myself in a long time.

My only goal for that challenge was to complete the challenge, and I did!

For my second challenge, my goal was to fit into my Disney jeans that I've held onto for 10 years hoping to fit into them again one day and now I do!

For my next challenge I want to lose a total of 50 lbs. That's only 10 lbs. away!

I tell everyone who will listen about the MAX. Just because I know it works. It's not just a gym or a fitness class or a diet. It's a way of life. Everyone is there to help you and cheer you on.

I never thought I'd get this far. I feel proud and I'm ready for my next challenge!

Norma Callahan

MAX Transformation story #100

Norma Callahan, MAX Transformation story
#100 – Before and After picture

Join the Ten Percent Club....

If you go to your local shopping mall and lined up 1,000 people I would bet that no more than 10 percent of those people would be at their ideal state of physical fitness. What is concerning is not how people look on the outside but what is happening on the inside. Heart disease, stroke, type two diabetes and cancer are all at an all-time high. Meanwhile, self-confidence is at an all-time low.

As Americans we are fortunate to live in a society that offers us the absolute best education. As smart as we are, we don't always seem to do smart things. Deep down inside we all know that the answer too many of the health problems we are facing today can be found in two simple solutions; proper nutrition and exercise. Yet we consistently reach for the quick fix in the next pill, diet fad or exercise machine!

Too make matters worse we have set our collective standard so low that it makes popping pills for everything from a stubbed toe and heart burn all the way too type two diabetes the norm.

It is time for us to take a close look at not only what we are doing too ourselves but what we are doing to our children and country along the way. The health habits, rituals and standards that we are handing down to the next generation are directing them straight down a path that leads too even poorer levels of health and a more concerning reliance on pills, medicines and machines.

Realize that if we are going to be the generation that truly makes a difference we each must first make a difference in our own lives. Every single one of us that steps up and begins to raise our personal standards in terms of health and fitness is setting an example. That example will slowly begin to open up the minds of the people around you. They too will begin making a difference in their own lives.

What does all this mean?

Think back to the example of the 1,0000 people in the mall. By taking your health and fitness into your own hands you are choosing to be part of the 10% club, the minority of Americans who take their health seriously. As you progress through your journey towards health the other 90% are going to try and pull you into their world. Remember the saying, "Misery Loves Company!" Stick to your goals, stay strong and stick with your commitment towards increased health. Before long you will begin to inspire others to join along and the 10% club will become the 15%, then 20% then 50% club......

Until one day it will tip and the large majority of Americans will raise their current health and wellness standards to new level of excellence. We will break our reliance on pills, medicines and quick fixes. Collectively enjoy increased levels of health, happiness and success. Resetting the collective health of our country and world at levels that we have possibly never seen before!

I have one last question for you.
So are you ready to step up and join the ten percent club?
-Bryan Klein, Founder of The MAX Challenge

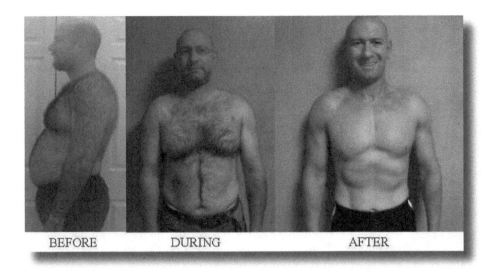

BEFORE DURING AFTER

Bryan Klein, Founder of the MAX Challenge – Before and After picture

If you have gotten to this page then you have read about 100 amazing people who have transformed their lives. I hope you realize the same opportunity is available to each and every one of us, it is just a matter of taking that first step forward and never turning back.

Let us help you get started with writing your next story. Here are a few helpful questions to help you get started:

1. What is it that you want? Be specific. For example, you want to lose 50lbs, when do you want to lose the weight by? Pick a specific date, leave no room for assumption. Another example would be you want to run a Marathon. What's the date? Where is the location? When is the final day to register?

2. What is standing in your way? What daily habits are keeping you from that goal? Be specific, this is the time to take ownership of what you want!

3. Identify new empowering rituals that will stop you from doing the things that were identified in the answer to question #2. Be specific.

The final step is to put the above plan into action! Make your story a reality, starting NOW!